DISTRIBUTION OF RIVER DOLPHINS

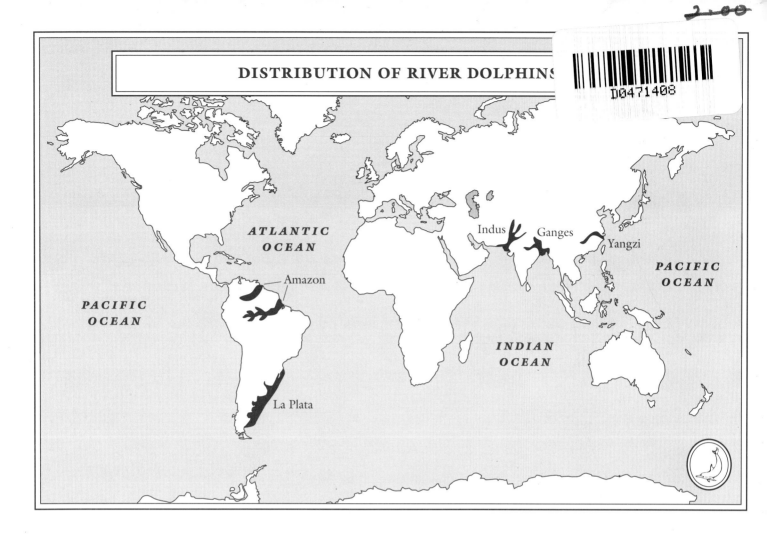

ATLANTIC OCEAN

Indus   Ganges   Yangzi

PACIFIC OCEAN

Amazon

PACIFIC OCEAN

INDIAN OCEAN

La Plata

DISTRIBUTION OF THE BOTTLENOSE DOLPHIN

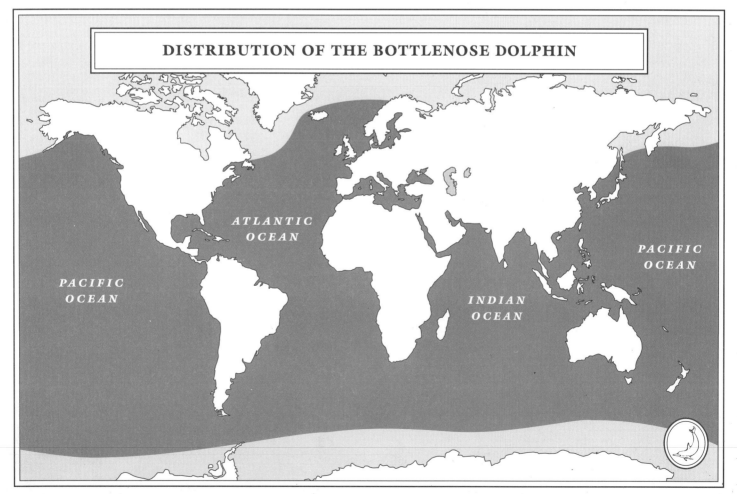

ATLANTIC OCEAN

PACIFIC OCEAN

PACIFIC OCEAN

INDIAN OCEAN

Dolphins

This book accompanies the ITV *In the Wild* television special
'Dolphins with Robin Williams' which is a Tigress Production for Meridian Broadcasting in
association with Thirteen/WNET.

Dolphins

CHRIS CATTON

Scientific Consultant: Bernd Würsig,
Director of the Marine Mammal Research Program,
Texas A & M University at Galveston

St. Martin's Press
New York

First published in Great Britain in 1995 by Boxtree Limited

3 5 7 9 10 8 6 4 2

Designed by David Rowley and Alan McKee
Colour Origination by Jade Reprographics, Essex
Printed in Great Britain by Bath Press Colourbooks, Glasgow

Boxtree Limited
Broadwall House
21 Broadwall
London SE1 9PL

A CIP catalogue entry for this book is
available from the British Library.

ISBN 1 85283 944 9

Front cover photograph by Jack Jackson
Back cover photograph by James D. Watt/Planet Earth Pictures

Contents

Acknowledgments

Many people have helped to make this book possible. The writer of a natural history book almost inevitably owes the greatest debt to the hundreds of researchers without whose many thousands of hours of patient observation we would still know almost nothing about the animals that share our planet. Much of the information in the book is taken from their scientific publications, and references to many of these can be found in the bibliography at the end of the book.

When I have been unable to locate up-to-date information I have often had to ask for help, and it has always been generously given. In particular I would like to thank Milo Gardner and Geoff Baldwin for helping to clarify my ideas about the place of dolphins in early mythology. Thanks are also due to David Fiedler, who drew my attention to the paper by Melitta Rabinovitch which is listed in the bibliography.

Marcos Cesar de Oliveira Santos provided information about Tiao, and Mats Amundin, Kathleen Dudzinski, Rob Harcourt, Suzanne Yin, Andrew Richards, Dagmar Fertl and Fredrik Hook supplied additional data about other sociable dolphins. Whitlow Au kindly answered questions about dolphin sonar.

Thanks are also due to Stacy Braslau-Schneck for sharing with me the results of her as yet unpublished work on how dolphins respond to the command 'Tandem Creative', and to Justin Weaver for allowing me to see the draft versions of work in progress which form the basis for the discussion on how dolphins might communicate, both of which are covered in the 'Senses' Section. Via the Internet I have also been in contact with several helpful contributors who have chosen to remain anonymous – thank you all, whoever you are.

International Dolphin Watch, and in particular Jane White, permitted me to reproduce their code of conduct for swimming with dolphins, which appears in the chapter, 'Meeting Dolphins for Ourselves'. Toni Frohoff shared with me the results of her research on captive-swim programs.

It is a pleasure to acknowledge the assistance of Bernd Würsig, who has kindly read through the whole manuscript, and Chris Sturtivant, who looked at the 'Senses' section. Their constructive criticism has much improved the end result. Nevertheless, all opinions and any remaining errors are entirely my responsibility.

Introduction

Since the beginning of time people have been interested in where the boundaries lie between humans and animals. We humans have defined ourselves as superior beings because we use tools, because we have a language, because we understand grammar, because we are self-aware – and in every case we have found that some animal somewhere challenges our definition by demonstrating the same abilities. One of the most recent challenges to our assumed supremacy has come from a most unlikely source. Not our close cousin, the chimpanzee, nor our more distant relative the gorilla; not in fact from an animal of the earth, but from a creature of the sea: the dolphin.

Throughout recorded history, dolphins have been endowed with symbolic potency. They are mythic animals; not in the sense that the unicorn and dragon are mythic, but in the sense that they have been chosen as religious symbols. With the growth of the science of biology over the last two centuries we have come to understand the real natures of other mythic animals, like the bear and the wolf, and in explaining them we have reduced their power. We have learned to hunt and trap them, to tame them, to make them dance or to keep them as companions. And where we have not had a use for them, we have hunted them to extinction. The lives of dolphins, on the other hand, are still shrouded in mystery.

The unknown is fertile ground for the imagination. Read the ancients, and you learn that dolphins are intermediaries between the worlds of the living and the dead. Read the writings of the New Age mystics, and you will discover that they are ambassadors from a planet of the star Sirius. If the dolphin is a symbol at all, the symbolism is clouded. We find them attractive, but it is hard to say why. Is it the fixed smile, the apparent playfulness, or simply their mastery of what to us is an alien medium that we most admire; or is it something else?

What we see in an animal is shaped by what we know about it. We think dolphins are intelligent, docile, friendly, co-operative and caring; we see them as we would like to see ourselves.

How true is this image, in the light of what we are now discovering about dolphin intelligence, communication and social behavior? The last thirty years have seen enormous growth in our knowledge about these

A young bottlenose dolphin swims beside its mother. To ancient sailors, the dolphin's mastery of the oceans must have seemed magical.

enigmatic creatures, yet the problems of studying dolphins are such that the gaps in that knowledge remain enormous. It is as if each new piece of the jigsaw, when fitted into place, serves only to show that the overall picture is larger, more varied and more complex than we first thought.

In consequence, the myths live on, although they change and bear new messages as we humans distance ourselves from the natural world. We are for the most part no longer in close contact with nature; yet every once in a while – through our pets, through television documentaries, or, most powerfully, through a once-in-a-lifetime interaction with a wild animal – we glimpse the connection that for most of human evolution has been a part of everyday experience. It is the aim of this book to explore this link between humans and the natural world, and between humans and dolphins in particular. Just why do we find dolphins so fascinating? What good does that fascination do us? And what harm might it do them?

Dolphins in the Human Mind

Dolphins in Ancient Mythology

Over 3,500 years old, the dolphin fresco from the Palace of Knossos in Crete is surprisingly realistic.

People who spend their lives at sea are superstitious. The sea itself tempts seafarers to become irrational. Before the days of the compass and the shipping forecast, the sea was indeed wildly unpredictable and dangerous. It is still terrifying and awesomely powerful, even with today's satellite positioning and sonar. To frightened, suggestible sailors, an inquisitive dolphin frolicking in the bow-wave must have seemed like a messenger from the gods. It is those seafarers, whose families never knew whether they would return alive, who gave us the first myths about the creatures.

The Greeks were among the first great seafaring nations, and the wealth of their civilization was built largely on their forays across the Mediterranean. It is not surprising, then, that dolphins appear frequently in Classical mythology – they are depicted, for example, on frescoes on the bathroom wall in the Palace of Knossos in Crete, which dates to 1600 BC – but it is through the writings of the Greek poets that most of the myths about dolphins are known to us today.

Opposite: *Apollo is often closely associated with dolphins, although what links them with the Greek god of the sun is not immediately obvious.*

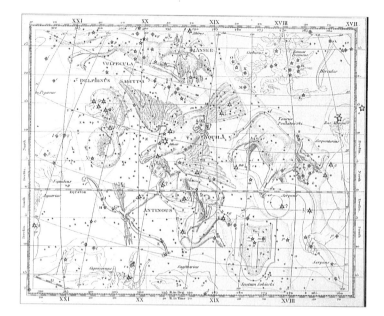

In the southern skies, the Greeks saw a dolphin in the stars. The constellation Delphinus disappears in winter and this may be connected with the dolphin's mythical journeys between the worlds of the living and the dead.

One of the earliest dolphin stories is Homer's 'Hymn to Apollo', which describes how the god Apollo founded the temple at Delphi after a journey which took him all over Greece in search of a suitable site. Eventually he chose a lonely cave nestling at the foot of Mount Parnassós, which was guarded by the dragoness Python, whom he slew with an arrow from his silver bow.

After killing the dragoness, Apollo set off to hijack a Cretan merchant ship, leaping aboard the boat in the guise of a dolphin. Terrified, the crew huddled below deck while the dolphin Apollo directed the winds to blow the ship right around the Greek coast and into the harbour below Delphi. Then, according to Homer's poem, the sun god instructed his hostages to live in the new temple and serve him as priests:

> And whereas I first, in the misty sea, sprung aboard the swift ship in the guise of a dolphin, therefore pray to me as Apollo Delphinus.

Like most myths, this is a story told in code. It is about the invasion of one culture by another; the replacement of the indigenous earth goddess Python, or Delphys, by the sun god Apollo; the overthrow of the mysterious, complex, female spirit of night by the bright, clear, logical, and pre-eminently masculine spirit of the sun. But why a dolphin? One possibility is that the dolphin was introduced in one of the first political whitewash jobs in recorded history. By the time the story came to be written down, Delphi was already growing rich. The Delphic Oracle was a respected prophetess, and worshippers were travelling from all over Greece and beyond to consult her and to ask for Apollo's blessing. The petitioners had also taken to leaving handsome donations. Could it be that the name Delphi, with its allusion to the previous occupant, Delphys, the earth mother, was an embarrassment? *Delphis*, the Greek for dolphin, is a very similar word to *delphys*, meaning womb. If the association with the old religion was proving awkward, what better solution than to introduce a dolphin into the story and explain away the name by a clever pun?

Like most reconstructions of this period of early Greek history, this is nothing more than pure speculation, and there are other less prosaic theories. The appearance of dolphins in earlier works of art at Knossos and elsewhere suggests that the dolphin already had a place in Cretan oral mythology, although the works of later writers and poets do not make it clear exactly what this was. The dolphin continued to feature in art and sculpture wherever the Greeks had influence, from Palestine and Mesopotamia in the east to Rome in the west, and later throughout the Roman Empire. Even in the rock city of Petra, miles from the sea and hidden in a cleft in the Jordanian desert, there is a carving of a dolphin.

Without a detailed written record it is difficult to know exactly what significance dolphins held for the Greeks. The sculptures, the mosaics, the beautifully engraved and painted pottery tell us that they were important, but not why. There are, however, some clues.

In many sculptures from the East, the dolphin is associated with Atargatis, the mother goddess, goddess of vegetation, nourisher of life and receiver of the dead who would be born again. In later myths, particularly in Roman literature, and again in art and statuary, it is the dolphin that carries souls to the 'Islands of the Blest', and around the Black Sea images of dolphins have been found in the hands of the dead, presumably to ensure their safe passage to the afterlife. Taken together these references seem to point to a deeper association with the processes of life, death and rebirth, perhaps linked to the dolphin's ability to pass between the air-breathing, living world of humans and the suffocating, terrifying world beneath the waves, which for the Greek sailors could easily be identified with the kingdom of the dead. Whatever the exact symbolism, it is clear that the dolphin is intimately involved with the fundamentals of human existence.

If the dolphin is implicated in some way in the transition between this world and the next it is no surprise to find that it is also associated with Dionysos, who himself dies and is reborn again each year in his role as the god of vegetation, and who was also worshipped at Delphi. Although most Greek writers refer to Delphi simply as the temple of Apollo, Plutarch is at pains to point out that the

worship of Dionysos was equally important at the site. He should know – he was one of the priests of Apollo at Delphi for many years.

Unfortunately for anyone trying to unravel the role of the dolphin in these Classical myths, Dionysos is one of the most enigmatic of the Greek gods. Conceived of an incestuous relationship between Zeus and his daughter Persephone, the baby Dionysos was killed by the Titans who ate all but his heart. On discovering the murder, Zeus killed the Titans with a bolt of lightning, swallowed the heart and gave birth to his own son.

This myth was apparently re-enacted in ceremonies that involved the slaughter of animals (and possibly human sacrifice too), and sexual practices

The lyre-playing Arion is rescued by a dolphin. By the late eighteenth century, when this etching was made, the portrayal of dolphins in works of art often bore little relation to the appearance of the real animal.

In Greek legend, Dionysos, god of vegetation and the vine, turns his captors into dolphins. The myth is illustrated on the Dionysos Cup (540 BC) by Exekias.

that would certainly find their way on to the front pages of the tabloid press if anyone tried to reinstate the cult of Dionysos today. After over 2,000 years of innuendo and cover-up, we cannot be sure what really happened in any of these ceremonies, and the part played by the dolphins has been long forgotten. Perhaps they carried Dionysos to and from the underworld; perhaps this is why several writers talk about dolphins disappearing each winter; perhaps this explains the name of the constellation Delphinus, the dolphin, which in Greece cannot be seen between the months of November and May. Today we can only guess.

The surviving story that links Dionysos with dolphins gives barely a hint of their mystical importance, though it does once again involve them in the transition between life and death. Dionysos is travelling in disguise on board a pirate ship when the sailors decide that instead of delivering their passenger safely home they will sell him into slavery in another town. Dionysos retaliates by driving the crew mad with hallucinations, at which they jump into the sea. They are saved from drowning only because they repent of their evil plan, at which Dionysos relents and turns them into dolphins.

This myth is often cited as the reason why, for many Greeks, killing a dolphin was an appalling crime. Dolphins were once human, and they retain human characteristics such as care for their young and sociability. According to the Greek poet Oppian, in his treatise on natural history:

> The hunting of dolphins is immoral and whoever willingly devises destruction for dolphins can no more draw nigh the gods as a welcome sacrificer nor touch their altars with clean hands but pollutes those who share the same roof with him.
>
> (*Halientica*, Bk 5)

After the founding of the temple at Delphi, many of Apollo's virtues came to be attributed to dolphins. As the god of shepherds and herdsmen, who traditionally whiled away the hours on the hills with a pipe, flute or lyre, he became by association the god of music,

The Dolphins of the Mediterranean

Several species of dolphin would be familiar to the sailors of the Mediterranean. Of these, the one most often seen in open water is the common dolphin (Delphinus delphis), a strikingly marked creature, dark above with a white belly and subtle patterns of light and dark bands on its flanks. It is found not only in the Mediterranean but in tropical and temperate waters around the world, and is probably the most numerous of all dolphins.

Another species common in the Mediterranean would have been the striped dolphin (Stenella coeruleoalba), a very distinctive animal whose white flanks are marked with an elegant gray stripe. This is probably the species depicted on the mosaic in the Palace of Knossos, which,

compared with many early representations of dolphins, is surprisingly accurate. However, it is less likely that either the striped or the common dolphin gave rise to the Classical stories of dolphin-riders – both prefer deep, open water and rarely come close to the shore.

Only two of the documented 'friendly' dolphins have been common dolphins. Most have been bottlenose dolphins (Tursiops truncatus). Their beak is longer than the beak of common dolphins, hence their name. This species is not generally as shy as the common dolphin, and is happier in shallow water. Because of this they have been the dolphins most commonly kept in captivity, and consequently they are the most thoroughly studied. Until recently, both common and bottlenose dolphins were caught for food in the Black Sea.

Above left: **The bottlenose dolphin, which often comes close to the shore, is the best-known of the species in the Mediterranean.** *Above right:* **Striped dolphins.** *Left:* **Although perhaps the most numerous of the world's dolphins, the common dolphin is not often seen, as it prefers deeper water.**

The Myths of the Boto

There are a number of interesting parallels between the Greek and Roman dolphin myths and the myths of the Amazon Basin. Here, some of the river dolphins are real dolphins, but some are enchanted beings who live in a city beneath the river. These dolphin beings are tricky customers, and delight in upsetting boats or damaging nets. They also steal human children.

In one story, for example, a woman takes her new-born baby down to the river's edge. Her husband arrives and asks for the child, and she hands it over and goes off to cook dinner. But when she goes back to collect the baby, her husband denies having taken it. The baby has been kidnapped by a dolphin in disguise.

Such stories no doubt have a practical purpose: told by a healer, they might ease a mother's mind and soften a tragic blow; told by the mother, they might be a traditional way of disguising infanticide. But these stories also echo the imagery of the Dionysos myth, with the dolphin taking the soul of the child not to the Isles of the Blest but to the enchanted city beneath the waves, where the dolphin beings and their guests live in luxury.

Thousands of miles separate Greece from the Amazon Basin, but these myths have not grown up in isolation. Although there may well have been indigenous Amerindian stories about dolphins, the stories told by villagers along the banks of the Amazon today are undoubtedly influenced by European myths which were brought to South America by Spanish and Portuguese settlers. Indeed in many of the stories, the dolphin being is a foreigner, shamelessly cunning, with no scruples about taking what does not belong to him.

The Amazonian myths are often explicit where other sources remain exasperatingly coy. Although many of the

Greek and Roman stories about dolphin-riders hint at a sexual element to the relationship between boys and dolphins, only in Aelian's tale of the dolphin-rider is this clearly stated (see page 17). In the lore of the Amazon, a dolphin will appear at a dance, or festa, and charm some young girl off her feet. Like the dolphins of Greek mythology, these gatecrashing dolphin beings are often attracted primarily by the music, and are sometimes expert musicians themselves. Although they appear in human form, dressed in fine clothes, they can be identified by an alert partygoer who knows their ways, because they never take their hats off – even when transformed they must keep their blow-holes covered. Once the lights go out and the music stops, the dolphin slips off with his chosen victim.

A female river dolphin, or Boto, and her calf. In the myths of the Amazon, the Boto is usually male.

and from this the dolphin of Greek myth gained a reputation as a music-lover. According to Pliny's *Natural History*:

The dolphin ... can be charmed by singing in harmony, and especially by the sound of the water–organ.

In a similar vein, the Greek writer Herodotus tells the story of Arion, a lyre-player from Methymna employed by Periander, King of Corinth. Arion is a talented and innovative musician whose performances around the Mediterranean have made him extremely rich. Sailing home from a lucrative tour of Italy to his native Corinth, his crew turn on him, threatening to

Modern Encounters

When wild dolphins choose to socialize with humans, they are often especially responsive to children.

Until relatively recently, the fanciful tales of the Greek and Roman poets and later the Christian biographers were not taken very seriously. Then, in the summer of 1955–6, a female bottlenose dolphin appeared in Hokianga Harbour at Opononi, New Zealand and made headlines around the world. She would swim close to the beach and play with small children, giving them rides on her back and attracting thousands of tourists to the town. Like the dolphin of myth, Opo was gentle with children, though she was inclined to give the shins of any adult attempting to impose himself a sharp smack with her tail. In March 1956, Opo was found dead in suspicious circumstances, and on the day after an Act of Parliament had been passed giving her legal protection. Interestingly, one of the earliest stories of friendly dolphins, told by the Roman author Pliny the Younger, has a similar ending: the local townspeople kill their dolphin to put an end to the hordes of visitors that have shattered their peaceful community.

Opposite: *In the clear waters of the Caribbean, a bottlenose dolphin investigates a scuba diver.*

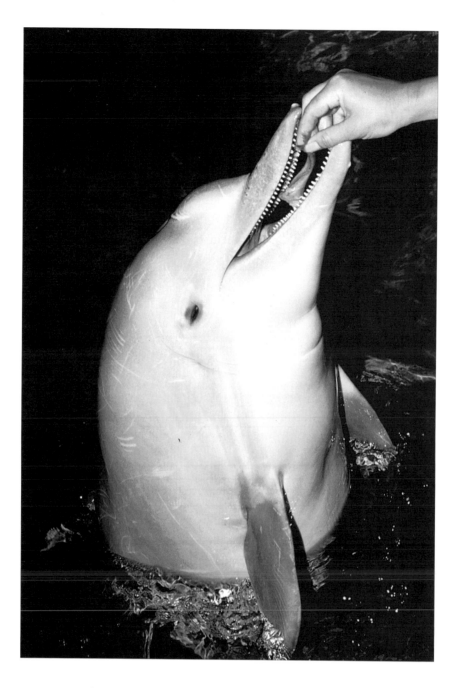

Dolphins carry a full set of teeth, which they use effectively in disputes amongst themselves. Humans that pester dolphins may be bitten, slapped with the tail or rammed.

Opo was not the first dolphin since the time of the early Christian saints to exhibit this sort of behavior, although previous encounters are rare and sparsely documented. The earliest for which records exist seems to be the case of a bottlenose dolphin, Gabriel, in English waters, reported in 1814. Between then and the appearance of Opo in 1954 only two or three other instances of dolphins interacting with humans are recorded. Presumably, the fishermen who met with friendly dolphins in the past were treated as unreliable witnesses – if they ever bothered to tell anyone outside their own community in the first place. In the last forty years, there have been fewer than fifty reliably documented incidents of dolphins accepting close social interaction with humans around the world.

One of the most carefully recorded cases is that of Donald, a male bottlenose who first began attracting attention to himself in March 1972 near a marine biology laboratory on the Isle of Man, between England and Ireland. Donald grew extremely friendly and would allow swimmers to hitch a ride by holding on to his dorsal fin, although he would never let anyone climb on his back. He also became mischievous, towing or overturning small boats, moving anchors, biting at paddles and generally creating havoc. The more excited humans became, the more exuberant Donald's behavior would be. Sometimes he would carry people out to sea, pushing them in the chest and preventing them from swimming back to shore, and he was even known to pin divers to the sea bed for a while. Yet on another occasion Donald rescued a diver in distress, supporting him gently on the surface and helping to carry him back to his boat.

It was inevitable that sooner or later a dolphin of such temperament would seriously injure someone. Donald and the other 'friendly' dolphins have generally been amazingly tolerant of humans, and their gentleness can make people forget that they are potentially dangerous. A dolphin is, after all, a 10ft- (3m-) long wild animal weighing perhaps over 500lbs (227kg) and equipped with a formidable set of teeth. In August 1994, a male bottlenose dolphin, named Tiao after the town of San Sebastiao where he was first spotted, began to socialize with people off the crowded beaches of the Brazilian coastal resorts around São

Below: *Tourists swimming with contained dolphins at Eilat, on the Red Sea. Around the world, humans are fascinated by dolphins.*

Overleaf: *Dolphins swim with amazing power and grace. The strength that lifts them clear of the water can also be used to protect themselves against sharks and humans.*

Dolphins to the Rescue

There are a number of recent stories about people being rescued by dolphins. Although most of these are, by their very nature, not supported by independent witnesses, there is no obvious reason to doubt them.

During World War II, six American airmen shot down in the middle of the Pacific Ocean said they had been rescued by a school of dolphins who pushed their tiny rubber dinghy to land. Not long after this, in 1949, an American woman was reportedly saved from drowning off the coast of Florida by a dolphin which pushed her back to the beach. Then there is the tale of the dolphins in the waters off the coast of Indonesia which pushed two crewmen from the shipwrecked tanker Elpina *to shore through shark-infested waters. Most remarkable of all is the rescue of a party of fishermen and their boat off the Brittany coast in 1993. A school of dolphins reportedly spent thirty minutes pushing the boat away from rocks on which it was about to flounder.*

While it may be that in each case the dolphins were deliberately intervening to save the lives of the humans involved, it is at least equally likely that they were simply playing, or responding to the struggles of the unfortunate victims more or less instinctively. Even before 300 BC, the Greek philosopher Aristotle was aware of the roots of this behavior:

On one occasion a shoal of dolphins, large and small, was seen, and certain of them, going at a little distance away, appeared swimming in underneath a little dead dolphin when it was sinking, and supporting it on their backs, trying out of compassion to prevent its being devoured by some other beast.

(Historia Animalium)

This phenomenon has since been observed many times. When a young dolphin is born, it is often pushed to the surface of the water by its mother, or by a close relative, so that it can take its first breath. It may be no more than this instinct that leads dolphins to behave as they do towards both their own dead young and drowning humans. When divers swimming alongside friendly dolphins have been pushed around in this way, the dolphin has been just as likely to push its toy out to sea as back towards the land. When a swimmer in real distress encounters a playful dolphin, the only outcome we get to hear about is a happy one.

A similarly down-to-earth explanation may also account for those cases in which dolphins are reported to have saved swimmers from shark attacks. One such incident occurred off the coast of New South Wales, Australia in 1989. Three teenagers were enjoying a day's surfing at the beach when one of them, seventeen-year-old Adam Maguire, was savaged by a 10ft (3m) shark, which bit him in the stomach and side and took a large chunk out of his surfboard. The boy was left badly wounded, and he would undoubtedly have died had it not been for a small school of dolphins swimming nearby which attacked the shark and drove it away. Although Adam owed his life to the dolphins, it seems likely that the creatures were more interested in getting rid of the threat to themselves and their young than in the fate of a human.

Paolo. As word got around, tourists began arriving in large numbers to play with him, and although he allowed himself to be stroked and seemed to enjoy swimming with people, not all the attention he received was welcome. At times, Tiao would be surrounded by up to thirty humans, some of them trying to climb on his back, tying things to his flippers, sticking things into his blow-hole, hitting him with sticks, or even trying to drag him out of the water to be photographed with the kids on the beach.

Tiao eventually began to fight back. In early December, he butted two men who were pestering him. One suffered a broken rib and the other died later in hospital from internal injuries. Immediately,

Opposite: *Our treatment of dolphins raises many questions about how humans should relate to animals. In performing dolphin shows, do we see an intelligent animal displaying mastery of its environment, or an arrogant human displaying dominance over nature?*

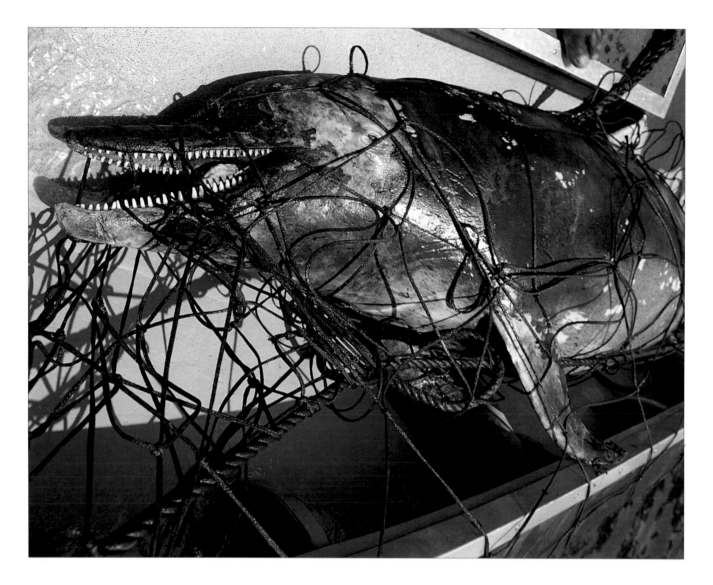

Dolphins are often attracted to fish caught in nets, but can easily become entangled themselves. Being air-breathing mammals, they quickly drown if they cannot struggle free and reach the surface.

the local press began running 'Killer Dolphin on the Loose' headlines. Local officials demanded:'The dolphin must be removed or killed. We can't lose the tourists' money because of a killer dolphin in the water.'

Having discovered that by being aggressive he could stop people hurting him, Tiao injured several more bathers as he attempted to defend himself. The exact number of casualties is unclear, since at least two of the six reported so far turn out to have been self-inflicted wounds by people hoping for a few moments fame and glory.

Despite the continuing problems, the demands for Tiao's death or capture faded away, perhaps because the local business community decided that they would make more money by leaving the dolphin in the water. Sections of the press could not resist the 'Killer Dolphin Reprieved' headline, but others helped to publicize and support a successful education campaign on the beach which quickly reduced the number of potentially dangerous encounters.

What is notable about this episode is not that a dolphin killed a swimmer who was tormenting him,

The dolphin's curving jaw-line gives the impression of a permanently fixed grin. This,
and their playful natures, may partly explain why humans find them so attractive.

but that this is the first known case of a wild dolphin killing a human being. Dolphins are immensely strong, and capable of swimming fast enough to lift themselves several metres clear of the water when they break the surface. By ramming with their beaks, they can even dispose of sharks that threaten their young. A human being stands no chance. Tiao was hardly the first dolphin to be subjected to torture by men (it is almost always men) trying to prove their ability to dominate anything that symbolizes the wild. Dolphins will usually tolerate a lot of ill treatment, responding with no more than a nudge with the beak, a gentle nip or a slap with the tail. But it seems that the endurance of even these benign and peaceful animals has a limit.

Why do some people see dolphins as symbolic of the wild, something to be 'tamed', exploited, put to human use when others see a tolerant, tranquil creature, an alien intelligence? These differing viewpoints reflect a wider dichotomy in human relations with animals throughout the consumptive world. The confusion about how humans relate to animals in general

Friendly dolphins

Date	Name	Location	Species	Sex
1800s	Old Tom and others	E Australia	Orcinus orca	(various)
1814	Gabriel	England	Tursiops truncatus	male
1888–1912	Pelorus Jack	NZ	Grampus griseus	male
1950s	Carolina Snowball	S Carolina	Tursiops truncatus	female
1953	Fish and Hoek	S Africa	Tursiops truncatus	female
1955–6	Opo	NZ	Tursiops truncatus	female
1965–6	Charlie	UK	Tursiops truncatus	female
1960s	Georgie Girl	Florida	Tursiops truncatus	female
1960s	Dolly	Florida	Tursiops truncatus	female
1961–2	Wallis	Australia	Tursiops truncatus	(uncertain)
1965	Nudgy	Florida	Tursiops truncatus	male
1972	Nina	Spain	Tursiops truncatus	female
1972–8	Donald (Beaky)	UK	Tursiops truncatus	male
1976–8	Sandy	Bahamas	Stenella plagiodon	male
1978–9	Horace	NZ	Tursiops truncatus	male
1978	Elsa	NZ	Delphinus delphis	female
1978–87	Jean-Louis	France	Tursiops truncatus	female
1979	Dobbie	Red Sea	Tursiops truncatus	male
1981	Whitianga	NZ	Delphinus delphis	female and baby
1981	Nudgy	Florida	Tursiops truncatus	male
1982–4	Percy	UK	Tursiops truncatus	male
1983	Costa Rican	Costa Rica	Tursiops truncatus	male
1984	Rampal	NZ	Delphinus delphis	male
1984	Tammy	NZ	Lagenorhynchus obscurus	male
1984–	Dorad (Funghie)	Ireland	Tursiops truncatus	male
1984–6	Simo II	UK	Tursiops truncatus	juv. male
1985–7	Romeo	Italy	Tursiops truncatus	male
1986	Fanny	France	Tursiops truncatus	female
1986	Pita	Belize	Tursiops truncatus	female
1988 approx.	Billy	Australia	(unknown)	(unknown)
1988	Jojo	Turks/Caicos	Tursiops truncatus	male
1988–1992	Freddie	Amble, UK	Tursiops truncatus	male
1988	Dolphy	France/Spain	Tursiops truncatus	female
1992	Maui	Kaikoura, NZ	Tursiops truncatus	female
1989–1992	Aihe★	Onekaka, NZ	Tursiops truncatus	female
1991	Flipper	Norway	Tursiops truncatus	male
1992–3	Solo	Southampton, UK	Delphinus delphis	female

★aka Goldie, Scarry, Madame

and dolphins in particular, is brought to life by Arthur Grimble in his book *A Pattern of Islands*. While working in what were then the Gilbert Islands in the South Pacific (now known as Kiribati), Grimble met a village elder who told him how some of the local people could 'call' dolphins. (Grimble actually describes them as porpoises, but since there are no porpoises within thousands of miles of these islands they are more likely to have been dolphins.) Few have the secret, but the hereditary dolphin-callers can go into a dream in which the spirit leaves their body and seeks out the 'porpoise folk' in their home under the western horizon. Grimble was skeptical, but arranged to be present at a ceremony:

> The hot hours dragged by, and nothing happened. Four o'clock passed. My faith was beginning to sag under the strain when a strangled howl burst from the dreamer's hut. I jumped round to see his cumbrous body come hurtling head first through the torn screens. He sprawled on his face, struggled up, and staggered into the open, a slobber of saliva shining on his chin. He stood awhile clawing at the air and whining on a queer high note like a puppy's. Then words came gulping out of him; '*Teirake! Teirake!* [Arise! Arise!] … They come, they come! … Our friends from the west.'

Sure enough, the dolphins arrived and, accompanied by shrieks and clapping from the villagers, swam towards the beach:

> They were moving towards us in extended order with spaces of two or three yards between them, as far as my eye could reach. So slowly they came, they seemed to be hung in a trance. Their leader drifted in hard by the dreamer's legs. He turned without a word to walk beside it as it idled towards the shallows.

The dolphins swam on until they grounded themselves on the beach, where they were lifted out of the wet sand and left to die, a spectacle which the author found disquieting:

> Men, women and children, leaping and posturing with shrieks that tore the sky, stripped off their garlands and flung them around the still bodies, in a sudden dreadful fury of boastfulness and derision. My mind still shrinks from that last scene – the raving humans, the beasts so triumphantly at rest.

It seems to me that this passage goes to the heart of the dilemma of how we as humans should relate to dolphins, and by extension to the other animals with which we share our world. Like most hunting peoples, the Gilbert Islanders believed in a contiguous relationship between man and nature. In this view of life, all nature is spiritual and aware, and animals give themselves willingly for food, provided that humans approach them with respect and humility.

For Arthur Grimble, as for anyone who does not share this cultural background, things are not so simple. If for a moment we put aside all doubt and accept that this story is accurate, then it defines dolphins as utterly exceptional animals with which some humans can share a truly mystical bond. If that is so, if there is even a chance that such a bond is possible, how can we buy fish in our supermarkets caught with nets that we know might have drowned dolphins? Without a guiding mythology, our reason, our biological needs, our greed and our intuition all pull in different directions.

There are signs that mankind is once again trying to address the fundamental problem of human relations with the natural world. The growth of the animal rights movement, the spread of vegetarianism and New Age philosophy and the tightening of animal welfare legislation all point to a questioning of the status quo. Dolphins, with their amiable, peaceable natures, their fixed smiles, their alien intelligence and their occasional seeking out of human contact, have come to represent the possibility of an alternative relationship between humans and animals. We shall return to this subject towards the end of the book, but before we can decide what value the dolphin has as a symbol in a post-modern society, we need to know a lot more about the dolphin as an animal.

What is a Dolphin?

The melon-headed whale has no beak, and although its common name suggests that it belongs to a different family, it is in fact a dolphin.

About 350 million years ago, a fish hauled itself out of some long-forgotten freshwater swamp and became the first backboned animal to colonize the land. With hindsight, the benefits of this bold evolutionary step are obvious. The land had already been invaded by plants and insects, so an enormous glut of food awaited the arrival of the first large grazers and predators. Once the new creatures had mastered breathing air and moving around on land, they went from strength to strength.

It is less clear why, some 300 million years later, the descendants of these colonizers should seek to get ahead in the evolutionary race by getting back into the water (see p. 36–37); and not just once, but on at least three separate occasions. First came what are supposed to be the ancestors of the whales and dolphins 65 million years ago, followed roughly 10 million years later by a descendant of the same ancestor that gave rise to the elephant and the rock hyrax.

Opposite: A dolphin in characteristic pose – but not all species of dolphin conform so well to the popular stereotype.

The Plight of the River Dolphins

The river dolphin is arguably the most primitive of all dolphins. It has a long, slender beak, and, unlike the marine variety, its neck is flexible because the vertebrae are not fused together. All five species have relatively poor eyesight, but the eyes of the Ganges and Indus dolphins have no lens at all and can perceive only light and dark.

Ganges dolphin (Platanista gangetica)
Distribution: *Ganges, Bramaputra and Karnaphuli rivers of India and Bangladesh.*
Population: *4,000–5,000.*

Indus dolphin, Indus susu, or bhulan (Platanista minor)
Population: *Around 500.*
Distribution: *Indus river, Pakistan.*

Baiji, or Yangzi, river dolphin (Lipotes vexillifer)
Population: *Around 100.*
Distribution: *Yangzi and Fuchun rivers, China.*

Boto, or Amazon, river dolphin (Inia geoffrensis)
Population: *Unknown, but probably the most numerous of the river dolphins.*
Distribution: *Amazon and Orinoco river systems of South America.*

Franciscana, or La Plata, dolphin (Pontoporia blainvillei)
Population: *Unknown.*
Distribution: *Coastal waters of eastern South America, from the Tropic of Capricorn to the Valdes Peninsula.*

All the river dolphins are increasingly threatened by human activity. Dam-building on the Indus and Ganges has divided the indigenous dolphins into small populations that cannot interbreed. Gold-mining in the Amazon Basin is causing serious pollution of some stretches of the river by mercury, which is used to purify

During the wet season, the forest along the banks of the river Amazon floods to a depth of several metres. Amazon river dolphins then leave the main river and swim between the trees.

the gold. In the Orinoco Basin, where the Amazon dolphin is still fairly common, there are ambitious plans for a series of dams to turn the interior of the country into a rice-growing area of world importance. Everywhere the effects of deforestation, and increased pollution by fertilizers and insecticides, are killing fish and reducing the dolphins' food supply. Most endangered of all is probably the Yangzi river dolphin. The Yangzi River is heavily overfished, and so food is scarce. In addition, major irrigation and flood-control projects in the lakes that join the river are changing the dolphin's habitat, and the ceaseless traffic inevitably results in the injury of animals by boat propellers.

Only the La Plata river dolphin is even moderately safe, since although it is more closely related to the other river dolphins than to the marine species, it in fact lives in the sea, along the coast of Argentina, Uruguay and Brazil. Although its habitat is consequently more secure, large numbers of La Plata dolphins are accidentally killed each year in gill nets set for sharks.

This second return to the sea led to the evolution of the dugongs and manatees. Not until 15 million years ago did the first carnivores make the same journey, evolving in their turn into the seals and sea lion.

It seems likely that in each case an animal that hunted for food in shallow marshes or lagoons became increasingly well adapted to life in the water, and less suited to the land. It has even been suggested that humans might have passed through a similar phase, which, some argue, may account for our shortage

Irrawaddy dolphin (Orcaella brevirostris)

Population: Unknown.

Distribution: From the Bay of Bengal, along the coasts of India, Pakistan, Burma, Vietnam and New Guinea to Northern Australia.

Despite its common name, the Irrawaddy dolphin is not a river dolphin, but a marine species. In fact, some taxonomists do not consider it a dolphin at all, arguing that it is more closely related to the beluga and narwhal. It is found in coastal waters from the Bay of Bengal to Northern Australia, and often enters large rivers. Like most coastal and river dolphins, it is suffering from human interference. In the Mekong River, for example, the local fishermen use hand-grenades left over from the conflict in Cambodia to stun fish, a practice which threatens the extinction of the local population.

Tucuxi (Sotalia fluviatilis)

Population: Unknown.

Distribution: Rivers and coastal waters along the east coast of South America, from the Orinoco River south to the Tropic of Cancer.

The tucuxi is equally at home in either fresh or salt water, and is found in several South American rivers including the Amazon and the Orinoco, where it lives alongside Amazon river dolphins. Although not closely related to the true river dolphins, some populations of tucuxi never leave fresh water at all, while other groups are exclusively marine.

The tucuxi is one of the smallest of all dolphins, growing to no more than 6.5ft (2m) in length. Consequently it is easily caught in fishermen's nets, and in parts of Brazil it is harpooned for shark bait and for human consumption.

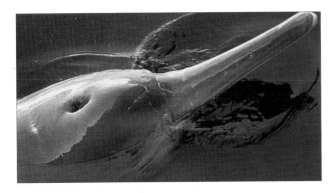

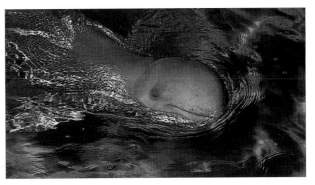

Above left: **A Yangzi river dolphin, probably close to extinction.**

Above right: **The Irrawaddy dolphin, threatened by the use of explosives for fishing in the Mekong river.**

Left: **Brazilian fishermen succeed in releasing a Tucuxi dolphin, captured by accident in a fishing net.**

of hair and upright stance. If this is true, humans never committed themselves to life in the water and returned to the land, their bodies retaining only tantalizing hints of what might have been an important, if brief, phase in our evolutionary history. For whales and dolphins, though, there was no turning back.

Probably soon after the ancestors of modern whales and dolphins first took to the sea, they split into two different lines. One line, which eventually gave rise to the great whales and their relatives,

Above: *The Amazon river dolphin, or Boto, is one of a group of dolphins that has adapted to life in fresh water.*

Right: *Long-finned pilot whales, like several large marine mammals that are commonly called whales actually belong to the dolphin family.*

became specialist filter feeders, while the other retained functional teeth. This was the forerunner of the toothed whales, a group which includes the dolphin, the sperm whale, the belukha, the narwhal, the beaked whale and the porpoise. Of these, only the porpoise is small enough to be easily confused with a dolphin.

Many American biologists used to make no vernacular distinction between dolphins and porpoises and referred to all small-toothed whales as porpoises. The habit apparently began in Florida, to avoid confusing the dolphin with the totally unrelated dolphin fish. Since there are no true porpoises in Florida waters, the nomenclature worked well locally, but it has caused quite a bit of misunderstanding elsewhere. The true porpoise belongs to a different family, and is distinguished from the dolphin by its less beak-like snout and its flattened teeth.

Just how many species of dolphins there are in the world today depends very much on who is counting them. Taxonomy – the study of relationships between different animals and the identification and naming of

The Evolution of Dolphins

Not long after the demise of the dinosaurs, the land mass that is now Southern Asia was covered by a warm, shallow sea. Around the marshy shores to the west of this sea roamed creatures known as mesonychians, descendants of the same group of animals that provided the distant ancestors of the gazelles, cattle, and horses. However, they were quite unlike the peaceful vegetarians their scions have become today. Similar to a modern wolf in general appearance but with five hoof-like toes on each foot instead of claws, they were probably also quite wolf-like in their manners.

The mesonychians once covered much of America, Europe and Asia. Some 65 million years ago, around the margins of the ancient Tethys Sea in the area that is now the Middle East and Southern Asia, one group became increasingly dependent on the abundant supply of food from the productive waters. Although they probably still returned to the land to mate and give birth (in much the same way as seals do today), this line became specialized aquatic mammals with teeth adapted to grasping and chopping up slippery fish. Their descendants slowly took over the role of marine predator vacated by reptiles like the ichthyosaurs and plesiosaurs, which became extinct with the dinosaurs.

Unlikely though it may seem, these hairy, hoofed wolves splashing about in the margins of the Tethys Sea are the probable ancestors of today's whales and dolphins.

This, at least, is the traditional view, although the evolution of whales and dolphins has always been one of the great puzzles of biology, and recent discoveries now suggest a rather different history. From studying the genetic material of a range of whales and dolphins, along with DNA from cows, pigs and camels, some biologists believe that the transition from land to water must have occurred much later. This line of inquiry indicates that whales and dolphins are actually much more closely related to cattle and antelopes than they are to the other even-toed hoofed mammals, pigs and camels. If this is true it means that cattle, whales and dolphins shared a common ancestor after the pigs and camels had already begun to evolve along different lines. Consequently, the ancestor of whales and dolphins could not have taken to the sea until around 45 to 49 million years ago.

This is a rather surprising discovery, not least because fossils looking remarkably like ancestral whales, which have been discovered in Africa and Pakistan, are thought to be much older than this – perhaps even 60 million years old. This may mean that whale-like animals have evolved twice, first from the ancient mesonychians to produce whale-like creatures that later became extinct, and then, much later, from a cow-like ancestor to give rise to the modern whales and dolphins. Alternatively, of course, it could be that the recent biochemical studies are flawed. The evolution and relationships of whales and dolphins remains a matter of confusion and debate among biologists.

Stephen Gooder (after Larry Foster, 1979)

species – is rarely an exact science, and with dolphins it is a particularly gray area. Take the five surviving species of river dolphins, for example. Several of the world's great river systems are home to these unusual freshwater dolphins, which have traditionally been considered to be quite different from the marine species. Taxonomists used to lump them together as one family, separate from the marine dolphins, but more recently, some have begun to argue that the river dolphins are in fact only distantly related to each other, that their similarities are the result of separate adaptations to a freshwater lifestyle, and that consequently each should have a family of its own.

It's not only the river dolphins which cause problems. The situation is much the same with the marine dolphins. The bottlenose dolphin has been split into twenty different species at one time or another, but is now generally recognized as a single species. On the other hand, common dolphins, which have for most of this century been deemed a single species, are now identified as two separate ones. Many of the different species that have been recognized at some point in the past may be nothing more than hybrids of relatively common species.

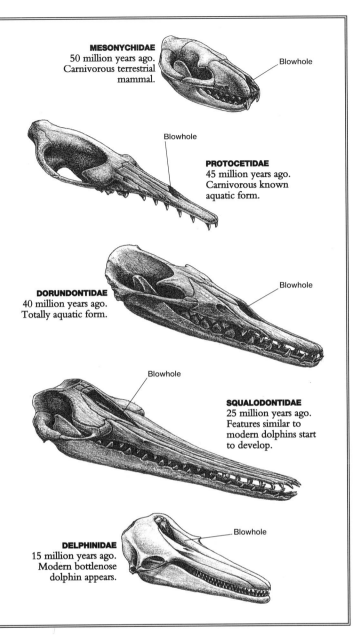

MESONYCHIDAE
50 million years ago.
Carnivorous terrestrial
mammal.

Blowhole

Blowhole

PROTOCETIDAE
45 million years ago.
Carnivorous known
aquatic form.

Blowhole

DORUNDONTIDAE
40 million years ago.
Totally aquatic form.

Blowhole

SQUALODONTIDAE
25 million years ago.
Features similar to
modern dolphins start
to develop.

Blowhole

DELPHINIDAE
15 million years ago.
Modern bottlenose
dolphin appears.

The orca, or killer whale, is the largest of the dolphins. True whales do not have teeth, but sift their prey through plates of baleen.

at the end of the book.

One point biologists do agree on is that the dolphin family definitely includes several animals commonly referred to as whales. The orca (or killer whale), the false killer whale, the melon-headed whale and the pilot whale are all dolphins: they are just much bigger than the other members of the family.

Whatever their exact origin, the whales and dolphins of today are very different from their ancient land-based ancestors. The hind limbs have all but disappeared, and movement through the water is achieved through the up-and-down movement of the tail flukes. The structure of the dolphin skeleton shows clearly that the flippers have evolved from a typical mammalian forelimb. The dolphin's flippers are not used to generate swimming power but as vanes, their pitch being varied to steer the animal through the water with astonishing agility. The teeth have evolved into interlocking rows of conical pegs suitable for holding slippery fish.

Perhaps most remarkably of all, the nostrils have migrated to the top of the head, allowing whales and dolphins to breathe while barely breaking the surface of the water. The dolphins' blowhole bears almost no

All of this confusion has arisen because it is so difficult to classify whales and dolphins. Many of them live only in the open oceans, and are therefore not easy to collect and preserve. Moreover, many of the techniques now being used to identify the relationships between such animals (DNA analysis and protein sequencing, for example) are still quite new, and the results are often contradictory. Only one thing is certain: any attempt to give a definitive classification of the thirty to forty species of dolphins that are currently recognized by scientists will be out of date very quickly. Instead, a simple list of common and Latin names in present use is given as an appendix

The teeth of the false killer whale are a formidable weapon, capable of tearing apart a whale much larger than themselves, or gripping a wriggling, slippery squid.

relation to the nostrils of land mammals. It is a semi-circular watertight valve, closed by a hinged flap, through which the dolphin can empty and refill its lungs in less than a fifth of a second. As the animal dives and the blow-hole closes, a slight trickle of water can enter, but this becomes trapped just beneath the blow-hole in a series of sacs closed by a second valve, the nasal plug. When the animal surfaces for its next breath, any water that has leaked into the sacs is blown out again.

As the dolphin breathes out, air leaves the blow-hole at speeds well over 100mph (161kph). This explosive exhalation clears the air above the water of spray as the dolphin breaks the surface. As the animal re-enters the water it pulls its head downwards, creating a small pocket of air above the blowhole from which it continues to inhale as the sea closes over the head.

Dolphins are superb divers. When they breathe, they exchange about 90 per cent of the air in their lungs – humans, in comparison, exchange only 12.5 per cent. Dolphins can also extract far more oxygen from that air than we can. Consequently, although a dolphin's lungs are not proportionally bigger than ours, some species can comfortably hold their breath and stay submerged for up to fifteen minutes.

The dolphin's body has also adapted to avoid the 'bends'. When a human returns to the surface after diving at even moderate depths, the fall in pressure can allow air bubbles to form in the blood and tissues. This can cause great pain, and cripple or even kill a diver who tries to surface too quickly. To prevent this from happening humans must pause regularly to allow the amount of oxygen dissolved in the blood to equilibrate with the pressure of air in the lungs. When a dolphin dives, however, its ribcage collapses completely, forcing the air under pressure out of the lungs and up into the windpipe and the complex chambers that lie below its blow-hole. Bottlenose dolphins can reach depths of over 1,640 ft (500m) without any ill effects at all, and pilot whales regularly dive to depths in excess of 1,960 ft (600m).

Countercurrent circulation

At first sight it appears that dolphins must inevitably lose much of their body heat through their flippers and flukes. These are less well protected with fat than the rest of the body, and they expose a relatively large surface area to the chilling water. The loss of heat from these extremities is much less than might be expected, though, thanks to the evolution of an amazing bit of plumbing. The arteries and veins of the flippers and flukes form a natural heat-exchanger, so that before heat can be lost to the surrounding seawater from the blood supplying the extremities, it is carried back into the body of the animal. The arteries taking blood away from the centre of the body are surrounded by a network of veins which cool the arterial blood and carry the heat back to the body's core.

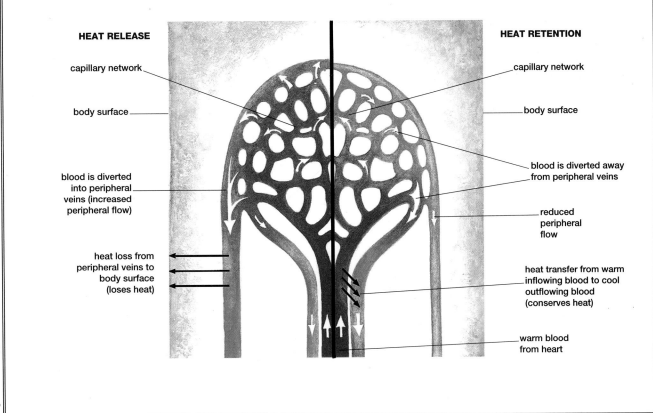

HEAT RELEASE

capillary network

body surface

blood is diverted into peripheral veins (increased peripheral flow)

heat loss from peripheral veins to body surface (loses heat)

HEAT RETENTION

capillary network

body surface

blood is diverted away from peripheral veins

reduced peripheral flow

heat transfer from warm inflowing blood to cool outflowing blood (conserves heat)

warm blood from heart

Stephen Gooder (after Pieter A. Folkens, 1987)

How a dolphin breathes

Approaching the surface, a dolphin begins to exhale.

Breathing out clears spray from around the blowhole.

As it breaks the surface, the dolphin immediately starts breathing in.

Stephen Gooder (after Jenny Wardrip, 1991)

The submerging dolphin creates an air pocket and continues to inhale.

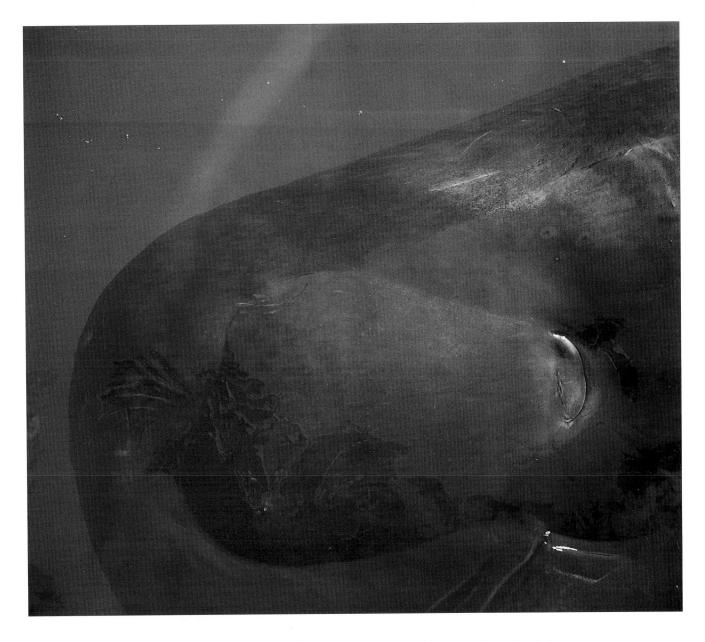

With their nostrils on top of their heads, whales and dolphins need only break the surface in order to breathe. As with this pilot whale, the blowhole of all dolphins is crescent-shaped and closed by a hinged flap.

The dolphin owes its ability to deflate its lungs in this way to the structure of its ribcage. Most of the ribs are not joined to the breastbone, and those that are are connected to it by long tendons. We know that this was an early evolutionary development because even ancient dolphin fossils show these characteristics. We can be less certain, however, about the structure of the soft tissues in the dolphins' ancestors, since these are not preserved in the fossil record.

As the dolphins' ancestors adapted to their new environment, their bodies became sleeker and more streamlined. Modern whales and dolphins have none of the irregular humps and bumps which typify land

Overleaf: *The sun glistens on the sleek, smooth skin of two bottlenose dolphins.*

Above: *When a killer whale breathes, it must empty and refill its lungs in a fraction of a second. As it exhales, air leaves the blowhole at speeds of well over 100mph.*
Opposite: *The sleek, streamlined body of a killer whale – a masterpiece of evolutionary engineering.*

mammals. Their ears do not protrude, and the male genitalia and female breasts are carried internally and extruded only when they are needed. The eyes of dolphins produce special 'dolphin tears', a slippery secretion which protects the eye against both foreign objects and infection and reduces friction between the surface of the eye and the surrounding seawater. Both whales and dolphins are practically hairless (they have retained a few hairs, or at least their follicles) and their skin is wonderfully smooth. This not only enables them to move easily through the water, but also reduces heat loss. Like humans, dolphins and whales maintain their core body temperature at around 37°C, but unlike us they have no body hair in which to trap an insulating layer of air. Since the sea is a better conductor of heat than air, marine mammals actually need rather better insulation than their relatives on the land. In dolphins and whales, this is achieved by a thick layer of fatty tissue beneath the skin, and (due to the advantage of a silky smooth skin) the reduced area of skin that is in contact with the water.

Senses

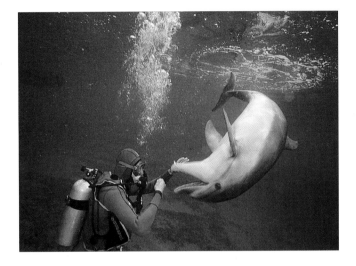

With its mouth open, a dolphin uses ultrasound to examine objects at close range.

Perhaps the least obvious but most remarkable of the modifications that allowed the evolving dolphin to survive in its new environment were the changes associated with the dolphin's methods of hearing and sound production. When the distant ancestors of dolphins first began to commit themselves to a life in the water, they must have had ears which, like our own, were suited to picking up sounds from the air. Although humans can hear quite well underwater, it is almost impossible for us to tell where a sound is coming from. The human brain uses several different clues to locate the source of a sound. Sounds coming from our left reach the left ear before the right, and we are particularly sensitive to this difference in timing. To locate a sound vertically in space, we rely on very subtle clues which include echoes from the ground and from our own shoulders.

Opposite: *One reason that dolphins seem to take an interest in human swimmers may be that, like them, we are air-breathing mammals. To a dolphin's ultrasound, our bodies may look similar to theirs.*

We also depend more than we realize on our experience. For example, if we are listening to a radio program with an airport scene, we build a mental picture in which the noise of cars comes from the ground and that of planes from the air, even though there are no clues on the soundtrack to tell us this is the case.

Most of the clues we use to identify and locate sounds are useless underwater. Sound travels about four times faster in water than it does in air, and so it becomes very difficult to distinguish its horizontal direction on the basis of the time at which the sound arrives. The greater speed of sound in water also distorts our subconscious ability to process the data we receive from echoes, so that we have very little idea of whether sound is coming from above or below. And of course we have not learned to hear in water, so we have hardly any experience on which to base the guesses we normally use to fill in the missing bits of information.

So how have dolphins overcome these problems? Although several biologists have spent most of their working lives trying to unravel the mysteries of the dolphin's hearing, the simple answer is that we do not really know for sure. Block off a dolphin's ears with suction cups and its ability to hear is hardly affected at all. The dolphin's external ears are extremely small, and it is quite possible that the canal which in land animals carries sound from the air to the surface of the eardrum is not functional in dolphins. Instead, sound may be carried from the water to the inner ear by a different route.

The most likely alternative path is the dolphin's lower jaw. It has been suggested that vibrations in the water are picked up by the jawbone and at a point where the bone becomes so thin that it is almost translucent. This back end of the jawbone is known as the pan bone (because it is shaped like a frying pan). Inside the pan lies a lump of fatty tissue that connects almost directly to the middle ear. In theory this certainly seems to be an effective route for

The dolphin's round, bulbous forehead is called the melon. It may serve to focus the dolphin's broadband clicks on to its target.

Echolocation

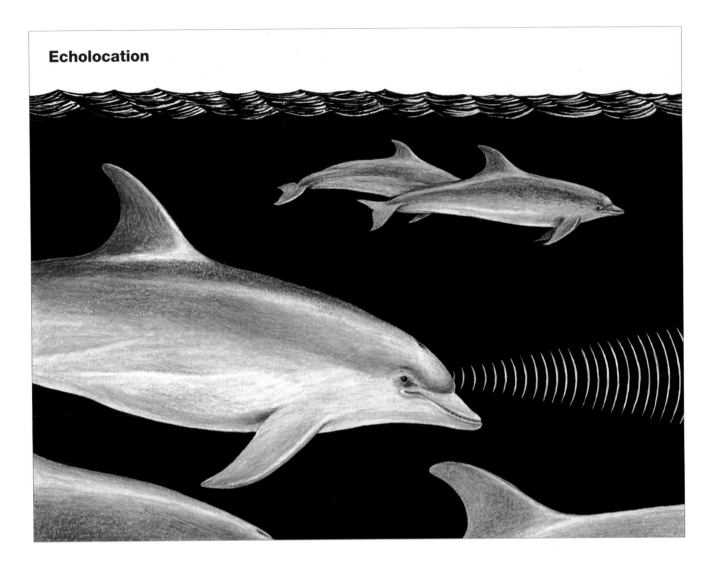

A dolphin swims with its jaw angled slightly downwards. Sound pulses emitted by the
nasal plug are focused by the melon, and projected directly forwards.

transmitting sound: both bone and fat are good sound-conductors, and since both are of about the same density as seawater, most of the sound striking the jaw would be carried to the inner ear with little being reflected. And if you cover a dolphin's lower jaw with a rubber jacket it does seem to have a lot of trouble with directional hearing.

The way in which dolphins produce the sounds they make is also the subject of debate. Most mammals produce sounds from the larynx (the Adam's apple in the human throat), where the vocal chords lie. These vibrate as air from the lungs is forced across

them, producing a sound. One thing we can be definite about is that dolphins use a different system, since they do not possess vocal chords. What is a matter of much debate is whether any of the sounds are produced in the larynx at all, or whether they are all produced by some other part of the dolphin's complicated airway.

Although most mammals use their larynx to produce the sounds, this may well not be true for dolphins. Biologists have used a whole range of extremely sophisticated equipment, most of it designed for use in human medicine, to examine what actually happens inside a dolphin as it makes a noise. All the results suggest that dolphin sounds are created by vibrations not in the throat, but in the nasal plug, which lies just below the animal's blow-hole. Either way, air expelled from the lungs sets something vibrating in the airway, but does not leave the body – when dolphins vocalize they do not usually blow bubbles. Instead, the air seems to be caught in a series of balloon-like structures between the nasal plug and the blow-hole, and returned to the lungs to be used again.

If, as seems likely, the nasal plug is indeed the source of dolphin sounds, this may explain the function of another peculiar part of the animal's anatomy which has long puzzled zoologists. The dolphin's rounded forehead, called the melon, contains a mass of fatty tissue that is quite unlike the blubber fat which insulates it against the cold and also serves as an energy store. In fact, the composition of the fatty tissue in the melon is unique, and even if the dolphin is malnourished it does not draw on this as a food source. It is hard to believe that a structure like the dolphin's melon, which represents a considerable amount of stored but untapped energy, does not have a function. Animals prosper in the evolutionary race only by being more efficient than their rivals, and the success of the dolphins appears to have been achieved in the face of stiff competition. If we accept that the melon must have a function, and if dolphin sounds are made by the nasal plug that lies behind the melon, that function might be to act as a lens to focus the sound, or perhaps as a transducer to facilitate the flow of sound from the nasal plug to the surrounding water.

Experiments show that the sounds produced by bottlenose dolphins are indeed focused into a narrow beam. Biologists who believe the nasal plug to be the source of dolphin sounds propose that this focusing is performed by the melon. Those few who favor the larynx as the sound source argue in favor of a different focusing mechanism which involves the lower jaw. Neither theory is entirely convincing. It may be that both mechanisms operate, each in different circumstances, with the nasal plug perhaps producing most types of sounds and the larynx the very high-frequency

clicks, although scientists are increasingly sceptical that the larynx plays any part in sound production.

The ability of dolphins to make a wide range of sounds and to hear clearly underwater is important because they rely on these faculties in almost every aspect of their daily lives. Dolphins use sound to communicate with each other, as do many other animals (we shall cover this in more detail in the next section), but they also use it for another, very different, purpose: echolocation.

For many years people had known that there was something mysterious about the way in which dolphins and their relatives perceived the world about them. Sperm whales, distant relatives of dolphins, feed largely on squid. With their jet-propelled escape routine, squid are not easy creatures to catch – even for an animal with perfect eyesight. Yet every once in a while whalers would come across a blind sperm whale which, despite its disability, had a full stomach and was as fat as any sighted whale. For the early seafarers, the only explanation was that whales and dolphins had supernatural powers.

Equally mysterious was the ability of dolphins to escape the nets laid by people trying to collect animals to display in captivity. Even in murky water the dolphins seemed to know where the nets were, and would swim though a gap before they could be closed. Biologists studying dolphins thought that perhaps they were using echolocation to find their way around, but this was no more than a guess.

In the 1950s, when it became possible to experiment with dolphins in captivity, researchers began to test this theory. One exercise involved hanging a series of poles in a pool on a dark and moonless night. The dolphins had no trouble at all avoiding these. In another experiment, a dolphin was trained to swim up and select its preferred food from two different species of fish. It could perform this task perfectly well, even in pitch darkness – and dolphins have no sense of smell. Such tests, however, did not exclude the possibility that dolphins could somehow see in very low light levels and were still relying on their eyesight. The matter was not settled beyond doubt until 1960, when a bottlenose dolphin fitted with suction cups over both eyes showed itself to be quite

capable of swimming through a maze of suspended poles. Researchers concluded that echolocation was indeed responsible for the dolphins' ability to identify objects in the dark.

The basic principle of echolocation is simple and not especially remarkable. The dolphin makes a click and listens for an echo, which tells it that there is something in the water. The time between the click and the echo tells the dolphin how far away it is. But dolphins can do more than detect and locate an object in open water: they can tell its size and the speed at which it is moving, they can distinguish

Left: *Dolphins can probably see as well in air as they do in water. As the iris closes in response to the bright light above the water, so the depth of field increases.*

Overleaf: *A killer-whale calf suckles from its mother. Early in life, a sense of taste may be important in helping calves locate their mother's breast.*

triangular, and rectangular shapes. It can locate a steel sphere the size of a walnut from over 230ft (70m) away, and detect larger objects within a range of up to 2,625ft (800m). And it can do all these things blindfolded. As Patrick Moore, a researcher for the US Navy's marine mammal program, puts it: 'to say that dolphins echolocate is like saying Michelangelo painted church ceilings.'

To us humans, who use sound primarily as a means of communication and not to find our way around, these abilities seem both extraordinary and rather alien. Yet while some of the dolphin's attributes are indeed amazing, much of the disparity between how a dolphin 'sees' through echolocation and how we see can be explained by fairly simple differences between light and sound.

Just as dolphins 'see' with reflected sound, humans see with reflected light. Light from the sun, for example, is reflected from the surface of an object and into our eyes. How we perceive the object depends partly on how much of the light is reflected, and from the pattern of light and shade we deduce its shape. If some part of the light spectrum is absorbed by the object and the rest reflected, it will appear to be colored, which gives us more clues about the identity of the object.

When soundwaves strike an object they behave rather differently. Some, like light waves, will be reflected from the surface of the object. Sound is reflected when it hits the boundary between two substances. How much sound is reflected, and how much continues to travel across the boundary and through the medium beyond, depends on the difference in the density of the two substances, and the speed at which sound travels in each of them. The greater the difference in density, the more sound is reflected. When it is small, most of the sound can

between different materials and they can sense an object on the ocean floor. They may even be able to use sound to kill their prey, as we will discuss later on.

A bottlenose dolphin can tell the difference between two spheres that vary in diameter by no more than 10 per cent and between circular,

continue straight on, to be reflected from surfaces inside an object.

Air and water have very different densities, and one of the strongest reflectors of sound traveling in water is a bubble of air. On the other hand, animal tissue, which is made up mostly of water, is a poor reflector of sound in water. When a dolphin uses echolocation to examine a fish it has a much clearer image of its swim bladder than of the whole animal. Just possibly, one reason why dolphins seem to be so inquisitive about humans might be that like them we are air-breathing mammals, and, being full of air, both human and dolphin lungs send back strong sound echoes. And remember that, while dolphins can hold their breath and dive to depths of over 1,000ft (305m) their lungs are actually about the same size as ours in proportion to the size of their bodies. To a dolphin, which probably relies as much on echolocation as on sight to perceive the world around it, our bodies may appear rather similar to theirs.

The dissimilar properties of light and sound can also explain how dolphins can 'see' some things that humans cannot. For example, the ability of sound to probe inside an object makes it quite simple for a dolphin to distinguish between a hollow water-filled cylinder and a solid one. It can even tell the difference between two hollow cylinders whose walls vary in thickness by only a couple of millimetres.

The image a dolphin gains of its environment through echolocation is often compared to that of an ultrasound scan, like those used in hospitals to look at an unborn child in its mother's womb. But although the basic mechanisms are similar, there are also important differences. In particular, medical ultrasound operates at much higher frequencies than the dolphin's echolocation system. While dolphins can produce and hear sounds that are beyond the range of human hearing these are still much lower in pitch than the sound produced by an ultrasound scanner. The use of these lower frequencies, which are not absorbed as quickly by seawater, allows dolphins to 'see' objects from much greater distances than medical ultrasound equipment could possibly cope with. On the other hand, while low-frequency sounds travel well through water, their echoes do not provide detailed informa-

tion because they are only reflected from relatively large objects. Consequently, dolphins cannot 'see' the same amount of fine detail.

Dolphins go part of the way towards overcoming this limitation by emitting sounds of many different frequencies, some of which humans can hear. They produce two main types of sound, clicks and whistles. The whistles are the more musical sounds, and are used for communication between animals, a subject we shall deal with later. The clicks, usually described as sounding like a rusty door hinge, are involved in the process of echolocation. They are 'broadband' sounds, which means that rather than being pitched at a particular frequency, they include a whole range of frequencies at once. It is as if a pianist, instead of using one finger to play a note, has slammed her entire forearm down on the keyboard. The resulting sound is not very musical, but it is well suited to the dolphins' purposes. The range of frequencies enables them to build up a more specific picture than they could from a single note. To get more information dolphins must employ higher-pitched sounds. They are known to emit sounds up to about nine octaves above Middle C, and may even be able to reach three octaves higher than that. These help the dolphin to 'see' more of the fine detail of what it is examining, if it can get close enough.

Most experiments in captivity suggest that dolphins tend to use a rather limited range of echolocation sounds, and do not adjust these much to suit the task at hand or the conditions. The situation in the wild may be rather more complex. A wild bottlenose dolphin swimming in open water repeatedly makes a sound with a pitch about three octaves above Middle C, well within the range of human hearing. Interestingly, this is quite close to the frequency chosen for most ships' sonars, and it is quite possible that the dolphin uses its own 'pings' in much the same way – to gauge the depth of the water, and to warn it of obstacles. Sounds at this pitch travel well through water, and the echoes can probably alert the dolphin to large obstructions several hundred yards away,

Opposite: *When dolphins swim close together, vision may be just as important as sound for communication.*

though not, of course, to the exact nature of the object.

Close to a target, a dolphin can learn more, at least in theory. Using the range of pitches in a broadband click, it would hear the frequencies at which the object begins to reverberate. These 'resonant frequencies' could act as a sort of sound signature, perhaps even allowing dolphins to identify a specific size or species of fish, even from a distance of some yards.

At very close quarters, dolphins may well use extremely high frequencies. They have often been observed to open their mouths around novel objects, apparently exploring them without touching them with their teeth or tongue. If the larynx is the source of these very high-pitched sounds, then this method of examination would beam sound directly from its source, with the echoes being picked up either from the teeth or at the back of the throat, where the fatty tissue runs into the inner ear, and which studies have clearly shown is sensitive to sound.

When bottlenose dolphins are examining targets at a range of yards rather than tens or hundreds of yards, they use high-frequency clicks, generally about eight octaves above Middle C. (Again, as these are clicks, we are not talking about a pure sound but a whole armful of notes.) At this pitch, the sound does not penetrate far through the water, but whatever the pitch of a sound, the louder it is the further away it can be heard. Dolphins using high-frequency sound to examine the detail of an object can amplify their echolocation clicks by focusing the sounds they produce into a narrow beam. At this sort of distance, a dolphin will often waggle its head from side to side while bombarding the target with clicks. It seems very likely that this head movement allows the dolphin to find the edges of the object it is scanning, and thus to get a good idea of its size, and perhaps its shape as well. It might also help the dolphin to decide whether the object is moving from side to side or is stationary in the water.

Another skill that might be useful to dolphins would be the ability to identify whether an echolocation target is moving towards or away from them. One way to do this would be to make use of the Doppler effect, a phenomenon named after the nineteenth-

century Austrian physicist Christian Doppler, who first explained it. The effect itself will be familiar to anyone who has listened to a police car going past at speed with its siren wailing. Inside the car, of course, the siren always sounds the same, but to someone in the street the note seems to be higher as the car approaches, and then to drop as it goes past. This is because, as the car comes closer, each successive wave of sound has slightly less distance to travel to reach the observer. The frequency at which the waves reach his ear consequently increases, and as the frequency increases so does the pitch. As the car moves away, each soundwave has slightly further to travel, and

both frequency and pitch begin to fall.

Horseshoe bats use the Doppler effect to gain information about the direction in which their prey is flying, and to locate the fluttering wings of moths on walls and cliffs. If the returning echo is lower in pitch than the original sound, the target is moving away; if the echo is higher, then it is moving towards the bat. But the echolocation sounds that bats make are not quite the same as those of dolphins. Horseshoe bat sound pulses are of a constant frequency and relatively pure tone, unlike the broadband clicks of dolphins, which are not well suited to extracting this kind of information. In fact, it may well be technically

Anomalies in the earth's magnetic field confuse animals that use an internal magnetic compass to navigate. This may be why whales and dolphins sometimes strand themselves on beaches.

impossible for dolphins to employ the Doppler effect, which is, perhaps, a little surprising: if the moving object were a shark, it would obviously be useful for the dolphin to know which way it was heading.

Our knowledge of how dolphins use their acoustic abilities is patchy. We know that they produce sounds with a wide range of pitches, and our understanding of physics allows us to make some guesses about what it is theoretically possible for dolphins to discover about their environment using these sounds. To some extent we can test these guesses by setting dolphins problems in which they must discriminate between, for example, a hollow and a solid sphere. A dolphin that is allowed to examine an object using echolocation can identify the same object from a visual identity parade of similar articles, and from this we can assume that it relates the sound picture it creates to the visual images it sees through its eyes.

This approach tells us a lot about what dolphins can know, but it will never tell us exactly how a dolphin processes the information; in other words, how it actually perceives the world. Does a dolphin 'see' a two-dimensional picture like that produced by medical ultrasound, or does it process the echoes it receives to create some sort of three-dimensional image? Since dolphins can easily tell whether an object they see with their eyes is the same as an object that they have previously examined with echolocation, we might assume that the systems produce similar images, but this is not necessarily true. Humans can perform the same sort of trick by handling objects when blindfolded, but the image we create in our minds by touching an object is definitely not the same as the one we have when we see it. In years to come people will certainly devise experiments through which we can learn a great deal more about dolphin perception, but ultimately many of the questions we are posing may be impossible to answer. Just as it is hopeless for a sighted human to try to explain vision to someone who has been blind from birth, so many details of the way in which dolphins perceive their environment through sound may always be beyond our knowing.

The dolphins' hearing and sound-production abilities have been extensively modified to suit their aquatic habitat. The change in their other senses has been less dramatic, but this does not mean that sight, touch, and taste are any less important for the modern dolphin than they were for its ancestors. Only the sense of smell has been lost. A young dolphin has tastebuds all over its tongue, which may be important in helping the suckling youngster find its mother's breast. As the animal grows older, these tastebuds disappear and are replaced by pits at the back of the tongue that may be sensitive to chemicals released by other dolphins in the school. Just like the scent marks left by many land mammals, these chemical messages may well signal an animal's emotional and reproductive state.

The dolphin has excellent peripheral vision, facilitated by the elliptical shape of its eye. The pupil is large, allowing the dolphin to see in the murky depths, but it can be closed to a narrow slit when the animal is at the surface. Dolphins can also change the shape of the lens in the eye so that they can see well both below water and in air. Many have some stereoscopic vision, and can probably judge distances in front of and below them quite accurately using sight alone. The eyes can also work independently, adjusting to different light levels and looking in different directions, rather like the eyes of a chameleon. Dolphins use vision to help pinpoint prey and avoid predators, but eyesight is perhaps most important in maintaining social contact within the school.

There is still much left to discover about the senses of dolphins. For instance, do they have a magnetic sense? We now know that some birds and also sharks can navigate using the earth's magnetic field to orient themselves, and minute particles of magnetite have been found in the brains of bottlenose and common dolphins, suggesting that perhaps they have a similar ability. There is also quite strong evidence that the peculiar habit of dolphins and whales stranding themselves on beaches may be the result of mistakes made in using their magnetic sense to navigate. Most live strandings occur near areas where the local magnetic field is distorted in some way, often by rocks containing deposits that are themselves rich in iron. These magnetic anomalies may interfere with the dolphin's ability to navigate by following geomagnetic contours.

These evolutionary developments – the sophisticated underwater sound-production and hearing system; the ability to dive to enormous depths, see underwater and navigate through the featureless oceans using the earth's magnetic field as a guide – have given whales and dolphins the tools to succeed in an environment that was alien to their ancestors. The next question is, how have they used these tools to establish themselves as successful marine predators?

Living Together

The Hunter and the Hunted

A school of bottlenose dolphins is not a stable social group. Tomorrow, the school may be a different size, as animals constantly move between groups.

As we have seen, millions of years of evolution have turned the dolphin from a land-based mammal with four legs into an efficient, streamlined predator of the open seas. Looking at dolphins today, it is fairly easy to see roughly the ways in which they have developed, but how did those early dolphins compete against other marine hunters which were already very well adapted to their environment? By the end of the 1960s, studies of dolphins in captivity had provided a wealth of information about their basic biology and their ability to find food and to look out for predators using a sophisticated form of sonar. This gave some useful clues to how these animals were adapted for their life at sea. In the early 1970s, and armed with this data from captive animals, biologists began to take to the seas themselves to look anew at how dolphins used their faculties in the wild.

Opposite: *Dolphins appear only fleetingly above the water's surface, travel at speed, and all look remarkably similar. Studying their social behavior is no easy task.*

A Reputation for Violence

The killer whale, or orca, is a large predator with a fearsome reputation, although in fact there is no evidence that these animals have ever harmed humans in the wild without having first been shot or harpooned. The name 'killer whale' in truth reflects the orca's ability to hound and kill true whales, often much larger than themselves. Because the term killer whale is open to misinterpretation, biologists who study them usually prefer to call them the orca, yet since this name derives from the Latin word for sea monster it is hardly any more flattering.

The orca's misconceived reputation as a killer of humans goes back many years. Here is one of Captain Scott's crew, relating an incident that occurred in 1911 on their ill-fated attempt to reach the South Pole:

I was a little late on the scene this morning and thereby witnessed a most extraordinary scene. Some six or seven killer whales, old and young, were skirting the fast floe edge ahead of the ship; they seemed excited and dived rapidly, almost touching the floe. As we watched, they suddenly appeared astern, raising their snouts out of water. I had heard weird stories of these beasts, but had never associated serious danger with them. Close to the water's edge lay the wire stern rope of the ship, and our two Esquimaux dogs were tethered to this. I did not think of connecting the movements of the whales with this fact, and seeing them so close I shouted to Ponting, who was standing abreast of the ship. He seized his camera and ran towards the floe edge to get a close picture of the beasts, which had momentarily disappeared. The next moment the whole floe under him and the dogs heaved up and split into fragments. One could hear the 'booming' noise as the whales rose

under the ice and struck it with their backs. Whale after whale rose under the ice, setting it rocking fiercely; luckily Ponting kept his feet and was able to fly to security. By an extraordinary chance also, the splits had been made around and between the dogs, so that neither of them fell into the water...

Of course, we have known well that killer whales continually skirt the edge of the floes and that they would undoubtedly snap up anyone who was unfortunate enough to fall into the water; but the fact that they were able to break ice of such thickness (at least 2½ft [76cm]) and that they could act in unison, was a revelation to us.

(L. Huxley, Scott's Last Expedition)

Would an orca actually snap up a human in the water, as Captain Scott's crew believed? Off the Valdés Peninsula in Argentina, orcas gather each year to prey on sea-lion pups. Along one short stretch of beach, a channel through the protective reef allows the orcas to swim close to the shore and grab pups playing in the surf. This predatory behavior was filmed for the BBC Television series 'The Trials of Life' by Paul Atkins and Mike de Gruy. They began shooting from the land, and watched as the whales cut through the water, snatched up a pup, smashed it on to the sand, carried it back out to sea, and then began tossing the body around like cats playing with a mouse. The sequence was very dramatic, but the film-makers felt they needed two more shots — an underwater shot of the whale approaching, and, perhaps even more dangerous, some footage from a sea-lion pup's point of view. Against the advice of almost everyone, Paul Atkins and Mike de Gruy decided to get into the water with the whales while they were attacking the beach, hoping that since humans are a good bit bigger than sea-lion pups they would be ignored by the whales. Paul Atkins took the job of filming the approach:

Since those early days, several different species of dolphin have been fairly extensively studied, and in this section we will need to jump around the world from one species to another as we attempt to unravel their lives. Although this may be a little confusing, it is important both to give a flavor of the range and variety of dolphin social systems and to fill in some of the gaps where details of behavior in any one species are unknown. Spotted and dusky dolphins, spinner dolphins and orcas all have their part to play in this

The idea was to hold on to the boat until the last minute and then swim out to the middle of the channel to meet the whale underwater. That was one of the more frightening experiences I can remember. I was hanging on to the boat with one hand, and in the other I held the camera. And I'm making a decision about when to swim out to meet this whale, waiting to the last minute. For a moment, I just couldn't make my hand let go of the boat.

The water visibility was 5–10ft [1.5–3m]. We wouldn't be able to see the whale until it was right on top of us. I looked up and watched the fin cutting towards me, just to get a bearing on it before I dipped under water. Talk about hearing the Jaws theme music. A huge 6ft [1.8m] fin coming at you gives you a primeval fear.

(BBC Wildlife Magazine, October 1990)

The whale headed straight past Paul, apparently concentrating on Mike de Gruy, who was lying in the surf:

There were no sea-lions around, so I knew that

Above left: **A killer whale swims up the attack channel and heads for the sea-lions on the beach.** *Above right:* **Once the sea-lion is in the jaws of a killer whale there is no escape. It will be carried back out to sea and torn apart by the rest of the pod.**

whatever it was homing in on was me. I was thinking, oh boy. What do I do? Do I get out of here now? Am I sacrificing myself? I hope they can find the camera and get a shot of the open mouth.

On this occasion, he need not have worried. The whale came to within about 10ft (3m), stuck its head out of the water, took a long, hard look — and then turned round and swam back out to sea.

In captivity though, orcas have sometimes proved less predictable. In 1991, two orcas at a dolphinarium in British Columbia dragged their keeper into the pool and drowned her. Amateur photographers wanting pictures of orcas would be well advised to stay out of the water and concentrate on shots above the surface.

story, but, perhaps predictably, one of the first species to be examined closely in its natural habitat was the familiar bottlenose dolphin.

As subjects for study in the wild, bottlenose dolphins have several advantages. They are relatively common, and although some are found out in the open oceans, many spend their entire lives close to the shore in fairly shallow water. As it was the species most often kept in captivity, biologists already knew more about the bottlenose dolphin than about any other group, and this knowledge would provide vital pointers in their attempt to piece together the way dolphins live.

The first thing the would-be students of dolphin behavior had to do was devise ways of watching, identifying and tracking wild dolphins. Early researchers would station themselves on clifftops with telescopes or surveyors' theodolites, a simple approach that made it possible to follow daily movement patterns and the larger-scale interactions within and between groups of animals. A group of Russian researchers, for example, working with bottlenose dolphins in the Black Sea, described several different forms of feeding behavior. The search for food would often begin with anything from six to twenty-two dolphins advancing in a line, like beaters at a pheasant shoot, or weaving a complex pattern through the water. Moving together on a broad front probably allows the group as a whole to scan a larger area for prey. When a shoal of fish was found, the dolphins would swim around them in a circle, forcing them into a tight ball. Shoaling in fish is often a defensive reaction to large predators, and it is thought to help them escape by making it difficult for the hunters to focus on any one individual. It may be because sight is not the most important sense for hunting dolphins that they do not appear to be troubled by their prey forming a defensive shaol. In fact, they even seem to encourage it, swimming round and round them and herding them closer and closer together. With the fish trapped by their own fear, and perhaps exhausted by the constant circling of the dolphins, the hunters then begin to dive through the centre of the shoal, picking off their victims.

This sort of feeding technique has been observed in other species of dolphin too. In Argentina, dusky dolphins feeding on shoals of southern anchovies in the shallow waters off Patagonia hunt in much the same way. They usually work in groups of eight or ten, but these small units are often in contact with others in the area, whistling to each other through the water. Once a group finds prey, the sounds the

The moment of impact. Among a pod of killer whales a few individuals are usually specialist hunters. They share their prey with their relatives.

Des dauphins prêtent assistance aux pêcheurs   D'après «La Nature»

Above: *In several widely scattered parts of the world, dolphins co-operate with local fishermen, and have done so for centuries.*

Right: *When they find a shoal of fish, dusky dolphins may call up reinforcements to help contain their prey and share the catch.*

dolphins make change, and, perhaps responding to these new sounds, other teams from the surrounding area begin to arrive. Larger groups may well be more efficient at herding fish, since smaller ones seem unable to keep the shoal trapped. So although the dolphins that discovered the shoal must share some of their catch, bringing in help probably means that there is more for everyone.

Similar hunting methods have been described by biologists studying orcas in the icy waters to the north of Norway. When feeding on shoaling fish like herrings, the orcas swim around and beneath the shoal, often leaping clear of the water or thrashing their tails on the surface, once again driving the shoal into a tight ball. Once the ball has formed, the orcas continue to keep the fish trapped by swimming close to the surface, their white undersides towards the shoal, and blowing large bubbles of air that probably create a 'ring of fear' that the fish dare not cross. Once the prey have been corralled, the orcas begin to stun them by slapping the underside of their flukes against the edge of the shoal, picking off the helpless victims one by one.

Bottlenose dolphins, too, have been seen to stun their prey using their flukes, 'kicking' fish through the air and catching them as they land again on the surface, but they may have another, even more formidable weapon. It has been suggested that bottlenose

dolphins can stun or perhaps even kill their prey with sound. There is no doubt that dolphins occasionally produce very loud noises, usually when they are angry. Some people who have swum with dolphins have reported discomfort that they have attributed to an intense burst of sound from the animal. And there

is certainly good evidence to show that dolphins can deliver bursts of sound loud enough to disorient or possibly even kill fish if sustained. Whether these bursts of sound are of long enough duration and of low enough frequency to have the required effect, is still a matter of some debate.

Another effective hunting technique is the 'wall'. Using this method, the dolphins do not surround their prey, but, strung out in a long line, they drive it either towards a waiting line of other dolphins, or against a shallow, sloping beach. Bottlenose dolphins have been observed driving fish on to the land in locations as far apart as the Black Sea, Portugal and South Carolina, forcing themselves to strand clear of the water among the floundering fish. As fish and dolphins slide back into the water, the prey are quickly gulped down. In Bull Creek, South Carolina, one group of dolphins regularly strand themselves within two hours of low tide, day and night, whenever the beaches are exposed. This activity appears to involve a degree of co-operation between the animals, with a single dolphin apparently leading the charge and four or five others joining in to drive the fish ashore. But if some sort of signal co-ordinating the attack passes between the dolphins before the hunt begins, researchers have been unable to identify it.

This form of hunting has resulted in several examples of co-operation between dolphins and human fisher-men. One of the best known of these takes place in the town of Laguna, near the southern tip of Brazil. According to local records, the practice dates back to 1847, and many of the fishermen involved today are the third generation of their families to fish with the dolphins. They use a circular nylon throw net, and position themselves in a line along the shore, each about a net's diameter from his neighbor. They stand and wait in the water, but the fishing cannot begin without the dolphins. About 200 dolphins live in the bay, and of these twenty-five to thirty work with the fishermen. They drive the fish towards the row of men, rolling over at the surface about five yards away from it, a movement that the fishermen take as their cue to throw their nets. Once the nets have been cast the fish panic, and a few no doubt turn directly into the jaws of the waiting dolphins. This teamwork is presumably to the benefit of both parties. Typically, the men catch 44lb (20kg) or more of mullet in a sin-gle session, which they sell in local markets. An adult bottlenose dolphin needs about 22–26lb (10–12kg) of mullet a day, and it certainly seems that while work-ing with the fishermen, they can catch this quantity with minimal effort.

A similar co-operative fishery can be found off the

A killer whale breaching. One reason for this behavior may be to contain their prey in a tight shoal, making it easier to catch.

coast of Mauritania in West Africa. In fact, the first records of this sort of fishing go back to ancient times. In his *Natural History*, the Roman writer Pliny the Elder describes humans and dolphins working together at Latera, in a way which could almost equally well describe the Brazilian fishery:

> At a fixed season a huge number of mullet rush through the narrow mouth of the marsh into the sea, after watching for a turn of the tide that prevents nets from being stretched across the channel.
>
> When the fishermen see this and a crowd collects, as they know the time and are keen on this sport, the whole population shouts as loudly as it can from the shore, calling on 'Snubnose' [a name traditionally given to dolphins by the Romans] for the finale of the show. The dolphins soon hear their wish and at once hurry to help.
>
> Their battle-line appears and immediately takes up position where the fray is to commence. They put themselves between the open sea and the shore and drive the mullet into shallow water. Then the fishermen set their nets and lift the fish out of the water with two-pronged spears.

If dolphins hunting for food are rewarded by joining forces with humans, what advantage do they gain by hunting with each other? If dusky dolphins really do call other groups to help confine their prey the inference is that this branch of the family tree, at least, really is co-operating in the hunt, performing as a team rather than acting individually.

In some cases it is clear that together dolphins can subdue prey that they would not be able to tackle alone. The orca is the largest of the dolphins, indeed one of the largest predators on earth, with the males reaching up to 31ft (9.5m) and the smaller females about 23ft (7.0m). Orcas feed on fish and squid, but their size allows them to take larger prey, too, including seals, birds, other species of dolphin and even large whales. The feeding behavior of orcas often features carefully synchronized group activity, very similar to the co-ordinated activities of social carnivores like lions and wolves on land. This is especially true when they are attacking big whales many times their own size. Naturally, it is rather unusual for anyone to stumble across an orca harrying a large whale, but when it has happened the pattern of the hunt and the eventual outcome have generally been much the same. The orcas begin by getting in front of their victim and slowing it down. Then, as some of the pod attack and bite at the whale's flanks, others swim above it, preventing it from coming to the surface for air. Eventually, the prey drowns, or is torn apart, and the pod feeds on the remains as they sink. When orcas are hunting seals in the shallows, one or two animals are specialists at the work and share their catch with the rest of the pod.

The degree of specialization and co-operation exhibited by orcas may set them apart from most of the smaller dolphins. Although the latter often appear to function as a team, they do not form such tightly knit social groupings, nor do they work together so closely when hunting. Even when hunting in groups, dolphins often seem to operate as individuals. Bottlenose dolphins do not always feed on shoaling fish, but often spend time searching the sea bed for solitary fish hiding beneath shelves of coral or buried in the sand. Yet even when foraging like this it is possible that there are advantages to working in a group. When a fish is disturbed by one dolphin but manages to escape it will be snapped up by another dolphin nearby. That said, when biologists have managed to watch dolphins foraging, missed catches appear to be quite rare, and each animal seems to act alone.

So there are situations where co-operative hunting, or at least hunting together, is an advantage to dolphins. For the orcas, and for other large dolphins that habitually hunt large prey, it may be that it is the single most important factor dictating the size and structure of the social group. But for the smaller dolphins, the benefits of hunting as a team seem limited at best, and indeed in many parts of the world individual dolphins of many different species seem to be perfectly content to lead largely solitary lives. If there are any great advantages to feeding together, these animals seem to be indifferent to them.

*A killer whale throws a southern sea-lion pup into the air after
grabbing it from the beach nearby.*

Probably one of the most common reasons why animals live in social groups is not that it improves their ability to find food, but that it helps them to avoid their enemies. More eyes on the look-out for danger make it more difficult for a predator to surprise them, and in the event of an attack being mounted, there is always a decent chance of finding cover in the centre of the group, in which case some other dolphin will be the victim. (Biologists charmingly call this the 'selfish herd effect'.)

Ever since dolphins first took to the sea, they have had to keep an eye open for one of the most efficient predators on the planet – the shark. Remains of dolphins have been found in the stomachs of tiger sharks, dusky sharks, bull sharks, and great white sharks, and it is more than likely that several other species also kill dolphins. In many parts of the world, a dolphin with a raw, gaping flesh wound is not an uncommon sight.

Sharks have been around for over 60 million years, which is longer than the dolphins, whichever of the theories about the origins of dolphins you prefer to believe. To judge from the fossil evidence they have remained more or less unchanged throughout that time. A modern shark can hear the low-frequency sounds of an animal splashing in the water from about a mile away. It can smell blood at over 1,312ft (400m). At close range it can use receptors on its snout to sense the minute electrical currents created by the nerves and muscles of its prey. When the ancestors of the modern dolphins first entered the water, it is likely that they operated exclusively in shallow lagoons and so avoided confrontations with ocean-going competitors like sharks. But if sharks were anywhere near as efficient at finding their prey 60 million years ago as they are today, how could the first dolphins have hoped to escape being eaten themselves, let alone compete, once they took to the open sea?

First-hand reports of meetings between dolphins and sharks suggest that on its own a dolphin has very little chance. One group of American scientists described what happened to a solitary dolphin after it had been released from a tuna net, a sight that must be all too familiar to tuna fishermen:

As she was swimming away, a large shark (about the same size as the 16ft [4.9m] chaser skiffs used in the fishing operation), with a robust body and sharply pointed head, came up from deep below the boat and bit the porpoise's [probably in fact spinner or spotted dolphin's] midsection. The porpoise sank slowly and was hit several more times by smaller sharks before what was left of her sank out of sight.

(From JS Leatherwood, WF Perrin, J LaGrange, 1973, 'Observations of Sharks Attacking Porpoises' (*Stenella spp.* and *Delphinus cf. D. delphis*), Naval Undersea Tech. Note, 908:1–7)

Compare this with the account of shark biologist Stewart Springer, who relates how a school of dolphins in the open sea used his party's boat to protect themselves against a shark attack. The dolphins had come close to the side of their ship. They looked tired, and some were injured. Thirty yards away, Springer could see the dim shapes of sharks:

There were six or eight quite young porpoises, not more than 3ft [0.9m] long, and these were

herded in close to the boat while some of the large ones patrolled the fringe of the porpoise school that now had our vessel to protect one flank.

Now and then a shark would come closer and one or more of the patrol porpoises would burst into a series of dashes. We could not see whether any contact was made between the porpoises and the sharks. The sharks always retreated but did not go away. Some of the patrol porpoises had been injured. Several were scarred and one had a badly shredded tail fin. It was easy to see that the porpoises were co-operating and that they were not only protecting their young but also were protecting each other.

(From American Institute of Biological Science, 1967, Conference on Shark–Porpoise Relationship Symposium Proceedings, Washington)

Eventually, a sharp squall began, and when it was over both dolphins and sharks had disappeared.

What these two accounts suggest is that although individual dolphins cannot defend themselves effectively against sharks, a larger school has a fighting chance. Dolphins may be able to kill sharks by ramming them with their beaks. Dolphins have occasionally been reported attacking sharks in the wild. Even though these reports are anecdotal, the readiness of dolphins to swim towards the source of danger, and the sharks' evasive response, certainly indicate that a fully grown male dolphin is something that even a large shark will treat with respect.

Aggression is not the dolphin's only defence against sharks, and it is probably not even the most important. Like all shoaling animals, dolphins gain protection from the visual confusion that a mass of twisting, flashing bodies generates. Kenneth Norris, whose studies over more than thirty years

Opposite: *By swimming close together, dolphins and other shoaling animals make it difficult for a predator to single out and attack a specific individual.*

have uncovered most of what we now know about the lives of spinner dolphins, has a theory about how this works.

In an attack sequence, the predator's [the shark's] eyes track the prey [the dolphin], but if the prey is moving fast across the visual field, the predator's eyes may not do so smoothly but progress in a series of jumps called saccades. When each jerk of such saccadic motion stops, the predator uses this fixed frame to make an automatic mental calculation of the course and

In daylight, spinner dolphins will often search out clear, inshore waters with a sandy bottom, where they can rest with no chance of being taken unawares by sharks which rely on sight to hunt their prey.

shark closing in for the kill tries to pick out a target. As the target tries to escape, the predator's eye follows it in a series of these saccades. But if the target swims past another dolphin, there is every chance that after the next jump, the shark's eye will settle on the wrong target. With the confusion of a panicking shoal, it is quite likely that this will happen again and again, making it impossible for the shark to calculate where the final point of impact with the prey will be, and so to anticipate the correct line of attack.

Kenneth Norris's studies suggest that the hours of daylight are the most dangerous for Hawaiian spinner dolphins. At night, the animals feed in deep water, probably relying on their sonar to detect sharks in the vicinity. In the darkness, sharks have no way of locating their prey that can compete with the dolphins' sonar, and although the dolphins may still be attacked by pygmy killer whales or orcas, they probably at least have the advantage that they can hear these animals coming. With the dawn, the dolphins move inshore to spend the day resting in shallow water, swimming in tight circles above a patch of clear, white sand. Dolphins cannot sleep in the way that we do, because their breathing is under conscious control. So if they lapsed into complete unconsciousness they would drown. Recording brainwaves in captive animals shows that a dolphin sleeps with only half its brain. While one side is asleep, the other remains awake; and even the sleeping side of the brain remains alert to sights and sounds. This ingenious arrangement means that even though Hawaiian spinner dolphins barely use their sonar at all while they are resting, the shoal can still watch for predators. It may well be that a period of quiet rest is essential for the tissues of the dolphin's sound-producing apparatus to recover from the huge mechanical stresses that they suffer every day. With their echolocation apparatus switched off, the patch of sand over which the dolphins choose to rest is probably important in providing a clear view of the surrounding waters, and giving no cover for a sneak attack by predators.

speed of the prey it sees before it. Remarkably, in between jumps the predator's consciousness shuts off and it knows nothing at all about its own jumping eye movements.

Faced with a shoal of identical-looking dolphins, a

Living in Groups

Scars discolor the skin of Risso's dolphin, leaving a permanent record of past encounters with others of its kind.

Whether they are forced together by the search for food or the need to avoid predators, the result is that many dolphins spend their entire lives within a few yards of others of their kind. Living in such close proximity shapes their social lives, although the exact details of these social lives are only now beginning to emerge. The distant observation from clifftops that makes it possible to follow daily movement patterns and the larger-scale interactions between groups of dolphins is woefully inadequate for getting the sort of precise information that allows us to really understand how dolphin societies work. For that, researchers need to be able to identify individuals, to follow them day after day and year after year, to learn how they are related and who spends time with whom. Only with this sort of detailed knowledge can we really begin to understand why animals behave in the way they do. This information is not only interesting in itself, but, in the case of dolphins, may one day be vital in developing plans to conserve them as their numbers decline.

Opposite: Killer whales 'spy-hopping'. The whales probably do this to look for seals on the ice, and then work together to try and knock them into the water where they can be eaten.

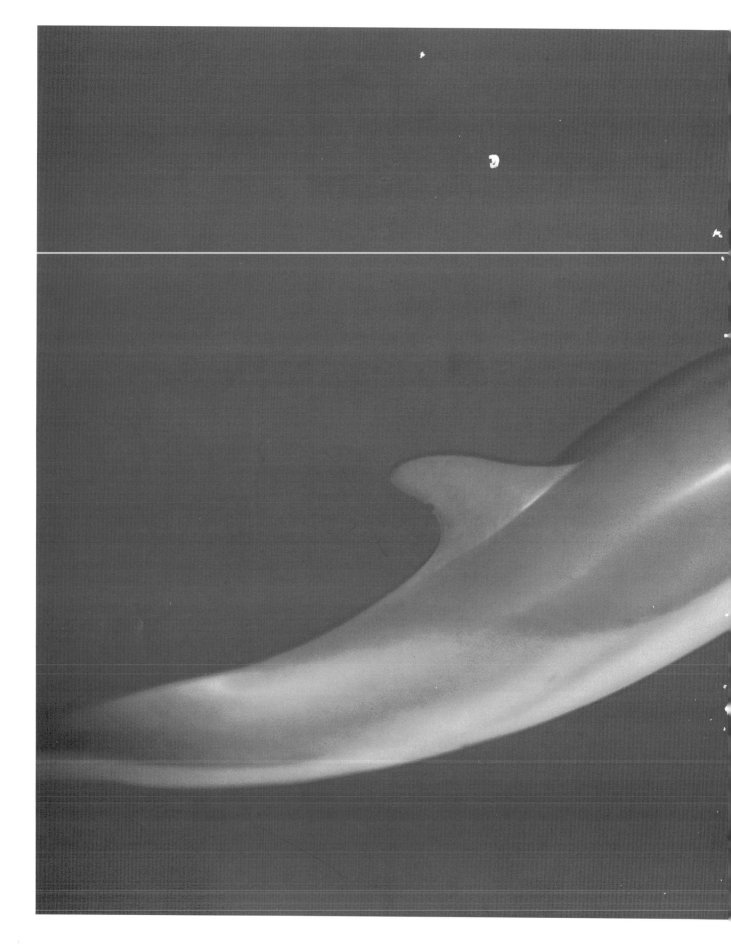

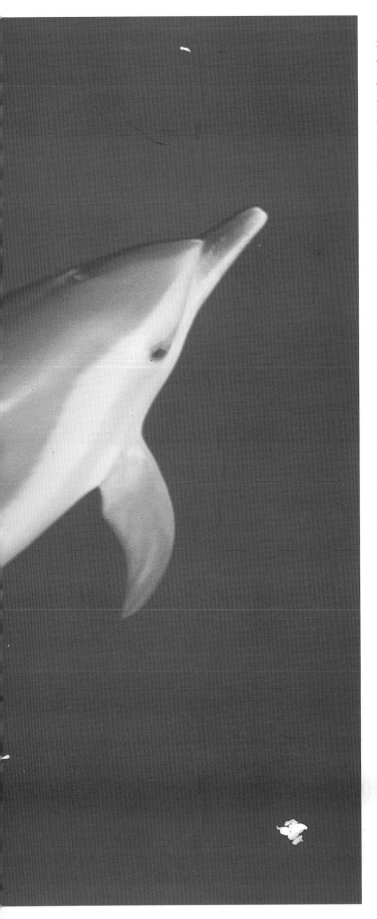

Identifying individual dolphins within the group is in fact quite simple, at least in principle. After the first year or two of life, dolphins begin to accumulate distinctive scars from brushes with sharks and other predators, or with others of their own species. Along with the natural variation in the shape of the dorsal fin, these scars can be used to identify individuals and scientific observers have built up photographic files on the hundreds of animals that make up their particular study group. In practice, though, this means sorting through thousands, perhaps tens of thousands, of slides, finding those that are in focus, those in which the image of the dolphin is big enough, and those that are well enough exposed to show the detail of the markings, and then matching these with similar photographs of the other side of the animal. Only once this great mug-shot file is pretty well complete can researchers start asking the really interesting questions about who spends time with whom, and why.

One of the first things to emerge from studies of this kind is that there is not just one type of dolphin society, but a whole range. Some are fluid, with animals constantly leaving and joining new social groupings. Others are stable, with the same animals spending most of their time together, changing partners only occasionally. And still others, like the orca pods, are perhaps the most rigidly static societies of any mammal, aquatic or terrestrial.

A pod of orcas may have up to fifty members which usually remain together for life, although pods may split into two if they grow too large, or merge with another if they become too small. The pod is made up of several family groups each led by one old matriarch. No one knows exactly what the maximum life expectancy is for killer whales in the wild, but it is estimated to be something like eighty to ninety years

Left: *The cookie cutter shark is more parasite than killer. It removes a small circle of skin from its victims, leaving scars that can help scientists to identify the individual dolphin.*

Overleaf: *Spotted dolphins appear to form reasonably stable societies, in which animals join and leave the core group only occasionally.*

for females and forty to fifty years for males. An adult female can bear a calf once every three years or so, although in practice once every eight years is the average. Gestation lasts for fifteen months, and the calf suckles for about a year, although it usually stays close to its mother for several years. In theory a pod could contain many generations of the same family, but half the young usually die before they are a year old, and so most pods contain only three or four generations.

This rigid social structure has interesting consequences, one of which is that the stable pods have a culture of their own. Biologists use the word 'culture' to describe behavior passed from generation to generation by learning, as opposed to innate behavior, which is inherited. In humans, one factor that differentiates one culture from another is language, and different orca cultures can be distinguished in the same way. Since a calf learns its repertoire of calls from its mother, and since animals never leave the pod to join another group of orcas, each pod tends to have its own dialect. These calls are apparently used to co-ordinate the behavior of the pod and to maintain contact with the other members. The studies by a Canadian research group in the waters off the west coast of North America show that here, at least, the pods are members of larger communities, and that pods within these communities tend to have similar dialects.

Two of the communities identified are resident: the northern community, which ranges north from Vancouver Island along the coast of British Columbia to Alaska, and the southern community which spreads south from Vancouver Island through Puget Sound and along the coast of Washington State. The third community is transient, and shows how varied the culture of orcas can be. The individual pods in this community travel farther, faster and in smaller groups. The itinerant social group specializes in hunting seals and whales, and since this requires stealth they are usually quieter than the residents. Often, though, they will call after a kill, and it is from their

A killer whale usually spends its entire life in the same pod, but the life expectancy for wild killer whales is unknown.

Dolphins We Know

A few species have become the focus of biological studies of dolphin behavior in the wild.

Spinner dolphin Stenella longirostris
Spinner dolphins are rather delicate, slender animals found throughout the temperate oceans. Some spend their lives near the shore, while other populations apparently never come close to land. Some schools may number over 2,000 animals. Spinner dolphins feed on small fish and squid, and are famous for the acrobatic spinning leaps that give them their name. Biologists studying the species believe that these leaps mark the edges of the dolphin school as it travels, and may also serve to check that the entire school is awake and ready to go before it moves off after a resting period.

Atlantic spotted dolphin Stenella frontalis, *Pantropical spotted dolphin* Stenella attenuata
As their names suggest, these dolphins are fairly easy to distinguish from others because they are spotted – or, at least, the adults are: the calves of both species are born without spots, and the markings increases with age. Both are somewhat similar in appearance, although the Atlantic spotted dolphin is more heavily built and has larger flippers, flukes and dorsal fin. The Pantropical spotted dolphin is found in tropical, subtropical and temperate waters throughout the world, while the Atlantic spotted dolphin is confined to the ocean from which it takes its name.

Dusky dolphin Lagenorhynchus obscurus
Dusky dolphins are exuberantly playful and acrobatic. They are found across the southern hemisphere, off the coasts of South America, South Africa and New Zealand. This species is rarely found more than 62 miles (100km) from shore. They usually travel in groups of ten to twelve, but are almost always in contact with an extended herd or school numbering up to 1,000 animals. The Pacific and Atlantic White-sided dolphins, Peale's dolphin and the Hourglass dolphin are all related species, the white-sided dolphins being found in cold northern waters, and the Hourglass dolphin and Peale's dolphin in Antarctic waters.

Long-finned pilot whale Globicephala melas, *Short-finned pilot whale* Globicephala macrorhynchus
Long-finned pilot whales weigh up to 6,614lb

(3,000kg) and reach lengths of over 20ft (6m), but, like the slightly smaller short-finned pilot whale, they are not true whales but dolphins. Both species dive to considerable depths to feed on squid, cod and other fish. The long-finned pilot whale is essentially a cold-water animal, and is found in temperate and subpolar waters in all oceans except the North Pacific. The short-finned pilot whale is found in tropical and subtropical waters.

Long-finned pilot whales are hunted for their meat by the Faroe Islanders, who drive pods of them into shallow water with boats and then kill them with a special knife designed to cut through the main artery in the neck. The practice has received a great deal of international criticism – the population of pilot whales is not known with any certainty and the hunt involves killing entire pods at a time. The effect on the genetics and structure of the population is therefore unknown. From a more emotive point of view, the killing is also gruesome, and the water turns red with blood as the whales are slaughtered.

Opposite: Sleek, spectacular and acrobatic, spinner dolphins have been affected by tuna fishing.
Top: Spotted dolphins are not easy to study because they rarely come close to the shore.
Above left: A dusky dolphin leaping. Dusky dolphins are found in the temperate, inshore waters of the southern hemisphere.
Above right: Short-finned pilot whales.

dialect that we know that the transient population from Alaska to California apparently comprises a single community. None of the three societies communicate or socialize with each other.

Since orcas never leave the pod in which they were born, all the animals within it are related. If they were not, it is doubtful whether the social system could possibly survive.

The reasons for this are rather subtle. Imagine for a moment a school of dolphins in which none of the animals are at all related. Now imagine that a dolphin arrives carrying a single gene that forces it to help other dolphins. (The idea that one gene alone might do this is probably ridiculous, but this is a theoretical argument, and the conclusion is useful.) Our helpful dolphin swims around doing good deeds. However, since none of the other dolphins carries the gene, our helpful dolphin spends a lot of time assisting others but gets nothing in return. Whether it is while defending the school against a shark, or through starving to death because it shared its food with others when times were hard, our helpful dolphin will be one of the first to die.

Obviously, in the case of orcas, co-operation allows the family to hunt prey that they could not hope to tackle individually, and to survive a lean period by sharing food. So how does this sort of co-operation evolve?

If our helpful dolphin is to survive, and continue to be altruistic, it must do one of two things. One is to make sure that it gets an equivalent amount of help in return. This is the basis of most human co-operation, and many social animals appear to strike similar deals with each other. Baboons, for example, will groom each other, often taking it in turns to groom

Left: *Killer-whale calves stay close to their mother for several years after birth. In this position, they can be drawn along by the mother in rather the same way that a cyclist can be dragged along in the slipstream of a large truck.*

Overleaf: *Like orcas, pilot whales spend their entire lives in the group into which they were born. Consequently, the members of a group are all closely related, and their society is stable and close-knit.*

and be groomed, as if to make sure that not too much energy is invested without ensuring a return. This is the problem with what is often called 'reciprocal altruism'. Having received aid, the other animal has the choice between returning the favor or not, and in the absence of ways of enforcing the principle of mutual assistance, cheats will prosper. This may be one reason why some dolphins help each other, but it is probably not the explanation for the dedicated co-operation of the orcas.

The second way in which a 'helpful' gene can survive is if all the animals in a group are closely related. Take a pod of orcas, for example. Because the pod are all related to each other, the consequences for a helpful pod member are rather different. Related animals are more likely to share the same genes, and a dolphin with a gene that forces it to care for others is likely to share that gene with its brothers and sisters, and with its parents. If the dolphin helps his relatives, he is promoting the spread of that gene. Because his relatives carry the same gene, they are likely to help him in return. So it is probably the rigid structure of orca society that allows them to share food and co-operate in the hunt.

The stability of the orca pods makes these animals relatively easy to study, at least in one respect. Once the individuals have been identified, (by variations in markings, or the shape of the dorsal fin), and once it has been established that the same orcas are always found together, the fundamental structure of the society becomes clear. With more fluid societies, like that of the bottlenose dolphin, things are not so straightforward. An individual swimming one day with one group may be with a completely different bunch of animals the next day. To make sense of the social system, researchers must not only be able to recognize the individuals, but to understand how they are related and to know their history.

To a practised eye, the shape of a dorsal fin and the pattern of markings can quickly identify individual killer whales within the group.

Rearing the Young
and Sexual Relations

Different fin-shapes and patterns of scars enable researchers to identify individual bottlenose dolphins, but getting a good photographic record of these athletic animals is not easy.

In 1970, Randall Wells and his colleagues began studying the behavior and ecology of the bottlenose dolphins along the west coast of Florida, near Sarasota, in what has since become one of the longest-running studies of dolphins anywhere. The researchers have built up a formidable quantity of data, including a file of photographs that enables them to recognize more than 1,200 individuals. Of these about 100 are permanently resident in the study area, and many of them have been temporarily captured and their size, sex, age, weight and general health recorded. By taking blood samples, the biologists can work out who is related to whom, and so build up a detailed picture of how bottlenose dolphin society functions.

Opposite: *Physical contact and sexual play are central to the social lives of dolphins.*

The bottlenose dolphins in Sarasota Bay have several distinct social groupings, and the strongest bonds of all are between a mother and her calf. From watching births in dolphinaria, biologists already knew that a dolphin calf is born tail first, and that the birth itself takes anything from a few minutes to several hours. Once the calf is born, it swims to the surface to take its first breath, sometimes helped by the mother or another female companion. The mother then guides the youngster to the travelling position alongside her and behind her head, where the young dolphin can ride with almost no effort, sucked along

An 'aunt' assists a mother and her calf.

until the birth of the next calf, which may not be for another two or three years, or in some cases even longer.

During the time that mother and calf spend together, the calf no doubt learns a great deal about its surroundings, about places to look for food, and how to work with other dolphins to catch it. Some of the time it will swim close to its mother, but as it grows it increasingly wanders off on its own, getting up to dolphin mischief only to be whacked with its mother's flukes or a pectoral fin and brought back into line. It is also during this period of infant dependency that the young dolphin learns to communicate.

As well as the mechanical-sounding echolocation clicks, dolphins produce a more musical range of sounds known as whistles. These whistles are used to communicate, and although we still know very little about the messages that pass between animals during whistling bouts, one particular sound has a very clear meaning. This is the animal's signature whistle, a brief burst that, like a fingerprint, is personal to every dolphin and identifies individuals to the other animals in their community. During the first few days after birth, a mother whistles to her calf continually, teaching it to recognize her call sign. Soon the calf begins to develop a signature whistle of its own, and to use this to keep in contact with its mother when it wanders off to explore. Although males tend to copy their mother's signature whistle, females usually develop a call of their own – possibly because it is more important for them to distinguish them from their female relatives later in life. Female bottlenose dolphins also learn the signature whistles of other females, and apparently use them to call these animals as if by name. But it is the males that develop the greatest talent for mimicry. One delightful theory about why this should be is that as they grow older males may imitate the whistles of their associates to suggest that they are part of a larger group than is really the case, and so avoid aggression from other males.

When the time comes for a young dolphin to leave its mother it joins a group of subadults. These are active, vibrant groups which intersperse the daily grind of finding food with bouts of leaping and chasing,

by the pressure wave created by its mother. Within a few hours, the youngster will begin to suckle, and although it will start feeding on fish after about six months, it may well continue to suckle from its mother for another three or four years. After the calf has been weaned, it usually remains with its mother

Above: *A spotted dolphin mother with her calf. Calves themselves are not spotted, but the intensity of the spotting increases as the dolphin grows older.*
Opposite: *Dolphins will often tolerate snorklers, and even come to seek out their company. But a snorkler cannot stay submerged for long and cannot keep up with dolphins as they hunt or socialize.*

rubbing and pushing, stroking and sex.

Dolphins begin having sex before they can possibly conceive. Calves as young as six weeks will copulate with older animals, including their own mothers. Males regularly couple with males; females rub genitals with females. Animals will stroke and fondle each other constantly. Often one dolphin will propel another around with its rostrum pushed firmly into its partner's genital slit, perhaps emitting a stimulating series of click sounds at the same time. Bottlenose dolphins which socialize with humans often demonstrate similar sexual interest in their playmates, which can be disturbing and confusing for both parties.

Very little of this sexual activity has anything to do with reproduction. Among bottlenose dolphins, reproductive behaviour tends to be seasonal. In the Sarasota Bay study area, for example, most fertile matings occur in late spring or early summer, and the calves are born a year later. So why do they do it? Most humans might be tempted to answer 'for fun', but this is not good enough. If it does not benefit the animals in some way, then evolutionary theory dictates that dolphins wasting time and energy on all this boisterous sexual play will lose out in the long run.

A full understanding of why dolphins indulge in so much sexual activity cannot be achieved by merely

varying degrees of success, from the crude to the elaborate. All have the advantage of allowing researchers to make notes easily as they watch, and to spend much longer 'underwater' than either a diver or snorkeller can. Most have the disadvantage that they make their occupants horribly seasick.

Using boats of this kind, Kenneth Norris and his team, who were studying spinner dolphins, investigated how much time dolphins spend in sexual play. The answer turned out to be almost unbelievable: a third of their waking hours. Patterns began to emerge in the behavior. A dolphin would caress one partner for a time, and then switch to start all over again with another. Sometimes a dozen or more dolphins would stroke each other at once, twisting and turning as they swam together at speed.

By analogy with land mammals, the most likely explanation for this frequent physical contact is that it serves to strengthen and confirm the relationships between members of the group. As with several land mammals, for example, mounting another animal may be a means of expressing dominance. Caressing may be the dolphin's equivalent of grooming in primates. Hours and hours of patient observation of baboons, chimpanzees and gorillas have shown that grooming sends signals about status and alliances, establishes and reinforces friendships, and is ultimately important in deciding who mates with whom. It is likely that similar messages are passed between dolphins as they nuzzle and stroke each other.

But what do they gain as a result? Like so many questions about dolphins, this exposes another hazy area where the little we know serves only to make us more aware of the true scale of our ignorance. Among land mammals, the purpose of dominance hierarchies, alliances and coalitions is usually to

Left: *When a young dolphin leaves its mother it joins a sub-adult group. These groups are often boisterous and engage in a great deal of social activity.*

Overleaf: *Sexual play and courtship behavior take up a great deal of time in all dolphin societies that have been studied so far. However, reproductive mating has rarely been observed in any species.*

snorkellers and are therefore able to watch from different angles, this advantage is offset by the disturbance caused to the dolphins by the bubbles from their breathing apparatus. Another alternative is to use some sort of boat which allows the occupants to see underwater. Several designs have been tried, with

With his beak in his partner's genital slit, and emitting a train of echolocation clicks, an adult male spotted dolphin stimulates a juvenile.

increase access to either food or sexual partners. Reproductive mating (as opposed to social coupling) between dolphins has rarely been observed in the wild. In the case of spinner dolphins, mating appears to be more or less promiscuous, with many males copulating in turn with a fertile female, and neither sex being able to influence who mates with whom.

Among bottlenose dolphins the situation is almost equally confused, although one aspect of their behavior is clearly quite different. As they become socially and sexually mature, the youngsters leave the subadult groups they joined after weaning, and males and females go their separate ways. Females join up with other females in 'bands', which typically include ten or so mothers and their most recent offspring. These

females do not spend all their time together, and the bands are fluid structures in which some individuals associate together frequently and others only rarely. Often a young female leaving a subadult group will rejoin the female band into which she was born, and genetic studies show that many bands consist of the females of families which have remained together for generations. This may explain why a female calf develops a signature whistle different from that of her mother. Otherwise, if she returned to her natal band, her own calf might well confuse its mother's call with its grandmother's. The tendency of females to reunite with their female relatives also explains the co-operation between female dolphins. It is not uncommon for a mother to leave her calf with a 'babysitter' from the

*Dolphins often court and copulate, but the females are infertile for
most of the year. Reproductive sexual activity, unlike social sex, is
rare.*

band, and during birth 'midwives' often assist the new mother, helping her to lift the newborn to the surface, or to position it at the mammary glands for feeding. It is probably not too fanciful to suggest that, as with humans, the most important contribution of these 'aunts' may be to provide comfort and reassurance to the young.

These roles are found in many species of dolphin. Female spotted dolphins often babysit groups of four or five calves while their parents are off foraging, calming youngsters who get too excited, and disciplining those who step out of line. There is evidence that among pilot whales (which, like orcas, are members of the dolphin family, despite their name), females continue to lactate well after breeding age,

and it has been suggested that these grandmothers are full-time wet-nurses who look after the calves while their mothers dive to great depths to feed. Like pods of orcas, schools of pilot whales are closely related families, and, in evolutionary terms, the grandmothers are not wasting valuable energy by feeding another animal's young, but ensuring the long-term survival of their own genes. So strong are the social ties binding a pilot whale school together that often if one animal accidentally strands itself on a beach, the other members of the pod will remain with it, eventually stranding and dying themselves, rather than leave their relative to suffer alone.

While female bottlenose dolphins spend most of their time after maturity with relatives of the same

sex, life for the males follows a different path. When they leave the subadult groups they either take up a solitary life or unite in coalitions of two or three which will often remain together for years. These alliances of male bottlenose dolphins have been studied in some detail by Rachel Smolker, Richard Conner and their associates at Monkey Mia, a small village on the shores of Shark Bay in Western Australia where since the 1960s, a few resident dolphins have regularly accepted fish from tourists wading in the shallows.

The research at Shark Bay has shown that the

Above: *The dolphins of Shark Bay. After years of study, biologists have uncovered the complex alliances that dictate the lives of these apparently carefree animals.*

Left: *At Monkey Mia, on the west coast of Australia, tourists have fed fish to wild dolphins for twenty years. In many countries though, the practice is illegal.*

leaping out of the water, spinning and somersaulting in perfect synchrony. Sometimes one of the males will make a distinctive popping sound, which seems to be the dolphin's equivalent of the command 'stay'. A female which ignores a popping male is likely to be bitten or thumped with the male's flukes or beak. But the herding males do not have things all their own way. They may be attacked by a rival alliance attempting to kidnap the prize. This leads to fierce underwater battles in which competing males slap at each other with their flukes and rake each other's flesh with their teeth.

It is reasonable to assume that the victorious males in these contests do indeed improve their chances of mating and passing on their genes. Since the females do not always seem to enjoy the attention of these roaming gangs, and frequently attempt to escape from them, the value of the coalition is obvious. Two or three males working together are more likely to succeed in fighting off challengers for their prize, and are also better able to prevent her from getting away. Nevertheless, kidnapping may not be the only method of courtship, or even the most important. Females are fertile several times during a breeding

coalitions of males work together to herd females which are in season. Presumably this herding behavior serves to keep other males away, and to give the males of the alliance, rather than outsiders, the best opportunity to mate with her. During herding, the males surround the female and display to her enthusiastically,

season, and do not necessarily conceive the first time they mate. It is not impossible that females can exercise some degree of 'choice' over who fathers their young. This selection need not be conscious – for example, a union which stresses the female might alter her hormone levels in such a way that the fertilized egg is less likely to implant in her uterus. Conversely, a quiet copulation with a longstanding 'friend' could be more likely to result in conception. Some males, and some male alliances, do indeed spend time 'befriending' females, swimming with them and stroking them in prolonged bouts of social stimulation, and some females seem quite content to swim with a particular male alliance while they are in season.

However much we speculate on the ways in which males might compete for the opportunity to mate with females, apart from the rather ostentatious battles between rival male alliances, there are very few hard facts to go on. What is clear is that the politics of dolphin society are almost as complex as our own. Males in particular must make difficult decisions about their alliance partners. To give a flavor of the Machiavellian contortions involved, here is Richard Connor describing one interaction:

> For those of us involved in the Shark Bay project, 19 August 1987 stands out as the exciting day we discovered the 'alliances of alliances'. Snubby, Sickle and Bibi were herding one of the tame females, Holey-fin, when a rival alliance, Trips and Bite, minus their usual partner Cetus, paid a visit to Monkey Mia. That was unusual enough in itself, so we expected fireworks immediately. But nothing happened. Trips and Bite just looked on as Snubby, Sickle and Bibi continued their excited displays around Holey-fin, then left. We followed.
>
> Nearly a mile offshore, they had joined up with their buddy Cetus, in addition to Real Notch and Hi, who were arch-enemies of Snubby, Sickle and Bibi. Real Notch and Hi were already herding the female Munch, but that evidently wasn't enough to keep them out

of a good fight with the males of Monkey Mia. Toward the park the two alliances traveled, and there, in front of startled tourists, they attacked and captured Holey-fin from their arch-rivals.

(*The Lives of Whales and Dolphins*)

Such machinations would seem to require a degree of reasoned cunning that we normally associate only with humans. Could this, perhaps, be the driving force behind the dolphins' legendary intelligence?

What evidence there is suggests that a substantial part of the dolphin's brain is involved in the storage, processing and interpretation of the massive quantity of information the animals receive from their echo-location activities. Although echolocation may be, by its very nature, a more complex way of picturing the world than sight, it is not obvious why dolphins require quite as much brain as they do to process their images. Bats manage to perform remarkable feats of echolocation with rather small brains. Like dolphins, they easily pinpoint even quite small stationary objects in complete darkness, and they can follow moving objects. Both dolphins and bats must use this information to move around in three dimensions and to locate their prey.

A larger brain may well help dolphins to build a more detailed and accurate image of their surroundings, but if bats can manage perfectly well flying in three dimensions at speed and catching minute prey, what is the evolutionary advantage for dolphins in being able to construct a more complex picture of their world? Given our rather crude understanding of how the brain works, it is certainly possible that once again we do not really know the full story. The demands of a complex social system seem to be the main driving force behind the evolution of large brains in land animals. The studies at Monkey Mia have shown that the dolphins' society may well be every bit as complex as that of a baboon or chimpanzee. Could the same pressures be at work here, in the sea, or is dolphin intelligence somehow different?

Dolphin Intelligence

Interpreting Information

When studying dolphins, it is not always easy to tell who is experimenting with who.

How smart are dolphins? Are they as intelligent as humans? Are they perhaps even more intelligent? It seems that we simply cannot resist playing with questions like this, even though it is obvious that they are meaningless: the intelligence of different animals is not something that can be measured like temperature or speed. Simply comparing the intelligence of two humans is a formidable task, perhaps an impossible one. Even intelligence tests designed to try to assess a range of skills and thereby to estimate the brainpower of people in effect tell us little more than how good the candidates are at answering the questions posed in these particular tests. How can we hope to obtain a sensible answer when we try to compare human and dolphin intelligence, unless all we expect to prove is that we are much better at solving human problems than they are? The point is neatly made by Douglas Adams, in *The Hitch-hiker's Guide to the Galaxy*.

Opposite: *Casual observation of dolphins in the wild gives little hint of their intelligence.*

Dolphin Tools

Humans have invented many reasons to justify planting themselves at the pinnacle of the pyramid of life. For a while, the most popular of these was that humans use tools. The first 'truly human' fossil is proudly named Homo habilis, (Able Man), and is supposedly distinguished from the apes that had gone before by the creature's ability to create and use tools.

This particular distinction between humans and animals began to look shaky almost as soon as it was suggested. First came the discovery of a finch on the Galapagos Islands which uses cactus spines to extract insect grubs from holes. More recently, the list of tool-using animals has grown rapidly. Sea otters have been found to break open shellfish with stones. Chimpanzees use small sticks to fish for termites inside termite mounds, and stones to break open palm nuts. Elephants scratch themselves with big sticks. There is even a species of ant that uses bits of leaf as a 'tray' to carry food back to its nest.

Since dolphins do not have arms and fingers, their ability to employ tools is obviously limited, but they manage. In Israel, a captive female bottlenose dolphin discovered how to catch fish for herself using small pieces of fish as bait. She would lie on her side near the bottom of her pool with her mouth open, gently holding the portions of fish between her open jaws. As small fish washed into the pool from the sea beyond were attracted to her bait, she would quickly snap them up.

There are two fascinating elements to this story. First, this was a captive animal, regularly fed a carefully balanced diet by her keepers, and so her inventiveness was not the result of desperate hunger. Secondly, within a few days three more animals had learned the same trick. Dolphins, not surprisingly, learn from each other as easily as they do from human trainers.

River dolphins – generally regarded as the most primitive and least intelligent of the dolphins – have also been observed to use tools, apparently purely for their own amusement. Captives in Duisberg Zoo in Germany have been seen blowing circles of bubbles underwater, and then swimming through them as they slowly rise. The same animals also built a 'bed' of bubbles by thrashing a pool-cleaning brush about on the surface and then quickly swimming into the resulting turbulence.

Inevitably, sightings of dolphins using tools in the wild are rare, but for the past ten years or so, the researchers at Shark Bay in Western Australia have been intrigued by a group of bottlenose dolphins that regularly carry around sponges, wearing them like gloves over their beaks. Although the researchers are not certain, they believe these sponges may be worn to protect the dolphin's beak from sharp rocks and the poisonous spines of stonefish as they forage for food on the sea bed.

Spotted dolphins playing with a scarf.

It is an important and popular fact that things are not always what they seem. For instance, on the planet Earth, man had always assumed that he was more intelligent than dolphins because he had achieved so much – the wheel, New York, wars and so on – whilst all the dolphins had ever done was muck about in water having a good time. But conversely, the dolphins had always believed that they were far more intelligent than man – for precisely the same reason.

It may be pointless to debate whether dolphins are smarter than humans, but it is perfectly reasonable to ask just what makes us think dolphins are intelligent

*Until the Marineland Aquarium began developing techniques
for maintaining dolphins in captivity, their abilities were
largely unknown.*

at all. As long ago as the seventeenth century, the biologist John Ray argued that the large size of the dolphin's brain, and its similarity to the human brain, suggested that the dolphin was an animal of 'more than ordinary wit and capacity'. But it was not until the 1940s, when people began studying dolphins in captivity, that the scale of this capacity started to become apparent.

Attempts to capture dolphins to display to the public began in the middle of the nineteenth century, although predictably most of these unfortunate animals died almost immediately. It was not until the opening of Marine Studios (later to become famous as Marineland of Florida) in 1938, that zoos and aquaria began to provide conditions in which dolphins could survive their captivity long enough for us to learn something about their abilities.

Marineland provided the first opportunity for a prolonged study of dolphins at close quarters. They quickly showed themselves to be playful, inventive and mischievous, deliberately teasing other animals that shared their aquarium. One youngster, known as Algie, would torment a grouper which lived in a crevice in the tank, tempting it with small pieces of squid and pulling the bait away as the grouper emerged to eat it. Another began harrying a pelican

*In captivity, dolphins have proved themselves to be intelligent, playful
and eager to please, abilities that have attracted the interests of biologists
and spawned a multi-million dollar industry.*

that shared the pool, chasing it and plucking out its feathers, though it never actually bit the bird itself. The captives also began to invent games for themselves, playing with their collection of pelican feathers, or with inflatable tyres provided by the aquarium staff. Even a live sea turtle might find itself being rolled around the bottom of the tank like a hoop or tossed into the air as if it were a ball.

Watching these games, the dolphin keepers at Marineland started to realize that dolphins were intelligent. It is hard to appreciate now that until dolphins were kept in captivity, almost nothing was known about their behavior or abilities. As we have seen, it was not until attempts to capture dolphins with nets for these aquaria failed so repeatedly that people even began to suspect that dolphins might be using echo-location to avoid the nets, and by extension perhaps to locate their prey. So even the ability of captive animals to fetch an inflatable rubber ring in much the same way as a dog fetches a stick came as quite a shock.

The sudden and rather surprising discovery that dolphins were smarter than the average fish prompted a wave of speculation. The biologist John Lilly opened his 1962 book *Man and Dolphin* with the lines:

Within the next decade or two the human species will establish communication with another species: non-human, alien, possibly extra-territorial, more probably marine; but definitely highly intelligent, perhaps even intelllectual.

Lilly began his scientific career by training as a medical doctor, and when World War II ended he began studying the electrical activity of monkey brains. It was through this background in neurophysiology that he became interested in dolphins. Shortly after the opening of Marineland, Lilly and a team of seven other investigators arrived in Florida to begin the first serious neurophysiological studies of a dolphin's brain. The study was not a huge success. Five animals died under anaesthetic, and the experiments were abandoned. But Lilly's interest in dolphins had been aroused, and he returned again two years later to use a new technique that allowed the electrical activity of the dolphin's brain to be studied without using a general anaesthetic. It was in this series of experiments, in 1957, that Lilly realized what the dolphin trainers at Marineland had already known for some time. Dolphins are clever.

In one experiment, Lilly inserted an electrode into the brain of a dolphin restrained in a tank. The tip of the electrode rested in a part of the organ where the dolphin experienced a pleasant sensation when a current was passed through the electrode. Lilly had already learned that, like a monkey, a dolphin would push a simple switch in order to stimulate this area for itself. Now he tried to train the dolphin to whistle in order to receive this stimulation as a reward. While he was doing this, the dolphin began to experiment with the biologist.

I noticed that he had added a new rule to our 'game'. He was raising the pitch of each subsequent whistle. Suddenly I couldn't hear the whistles any more but I could see the individual twitches of the blow-hole. Apparently he was whistling at frequencies so high that I could not hear them. I stopped rewarding him for each twitch. He then emitted two more 'supersonic'

Once it became possible to keep dolphins in captivity, the study of their intelligence and their abilities became relatively simple.

short twitches, and with the third twitch I could once more hear the whistles and rewarded him. From that time on he did not go out of my acoustic range. He had determined what my hearing range was, and stayed within it for the next few hours.

(Man and Dolphin)

At about the same time, Lilly noticed the ability of dolphins to mimic the human voice. It was experiences like these that began to persuade him that dolphins might be 'as intelligent as man'. He began a program to study the possibility of communication between humans and dolphins.

Lilly's revolutionary ideas were widely publicized in the late 1950s and early 1960s. He went on to set up a formal study of the dolphin's faculty for mimicry, and later to build a computer system to translate inputs at a keyboard into sounds that dolphins can hear. His work has since been severely criticized for its lack of scientific rigor, and the results were generally disappointing, certainly when measured against the early hopes of meaningful communication between humans and dolphins 'within the next decade or two'. Nevertheless, Lilly's early studies did have one very important effect. By sticking his neck out and giving voice to such outlandish opinions, he made those which followed seem fairly moderate by comparison.

Without any doubt the most significant work continuing these basic themes has been that done by Louis M. Herman and his colleagues at the Kewalo Basin Marine Mammal Laboratory in Hawaii. Since 1979, Louis Herman has worked with two captive female bottlenose dolphins named Phoenix and Akeakamai. Phoenix has been trained to understand computer-generated whistles, and Akeakamai to understand a form of sign language. In one experiment, for example, Phoenix was taught to associate different whistles with different objects – a ball, a hoop and a frisbee. When shown each article after this initial training, the dolphin would reliably respond with the correct whistle.

This in itself is not particularly remarkable, but it was only the beginning. Both dolphins can also comprehend sentences like 'Ball fetch hoop,' meaning 'Take the ball to the hoop.' To understand a whole phrase like this, the dolphin must be able to do two things. First, it must be able to distinguish between nouns and verbs – words for things, and words for doing things. Second, and much more difficult, it must understand the significance of the order of words, or syntax. There is, of course, a difference between 'Ball fetch hoop,' ('Take the ball to the hoop'), and 'Hoop fetch ball' ('Take the hoop to the ball').

To be quite sure that this ability to understand syntax was real, Herman's group trained each of their dolphins to interpret the word order differently. For Phoenix, the instruction 'Ball fetch hoop' means take the ball to the hoop, but Akeakamai must be told 'Hoop ball fetch' to get her to do the same. Both animals performed their tasks equally well. Furthermore, they were able to interpret the words they had learned when these were presented in a different sequence, following the new instructions almost as successfully as they did the familiar ones.

The researchers have also shown that dolphins are capable of abstract thought, another ability long believed to be exclusively human. In these experiments Akeakamai was presented with two switches which she could press with her beak, one for yes, and one for no. When asked, 'Is there a ball in the tank?' Akeakamai usually gave the right answer. This would require the dolphin to go through a complex mental process along the lines of 'What is a ball, oh yes, one of those round things.' It would need to know what the object was even though it wasn't there, and create some sort of mental image to match.

Phoenix and Akeakamai have each learned a vocabulary of about sixty words which their trainers can use to construct up to 2,000 different sentences, all of which the dolphins can understand. This may not be communication between human and alien intelligence at the level John Lilly had in mind in the 1950s, but it is astonishing nonetheless. Researchers working with primates have only recently managed to show that these animals, our closest relatives, can interpret the syntax of a sentence.

Another area of dolphin intelligence under investigation is whether or not the animals are aware of themselves as individuals. One procedure which has been used to discover if monkeys and apes are self-aware is the so-called mirror test. If a sleeping chimpanzee has a spot of paint dabbed on its forehead and then some time later is allowed to see its reflection in a mirror, it will immediately attempt to pick off the paint. Orang-utans also pass this test of self-awareness, whereas monkeys regularly fail it, often attacking the image as an intruder. Elephants, the other contenders for superior intellect, generally try to walk through the mirror.

Ken Marten, working at the Sea Life Park in Hawaii, has attempted to carry out similar experiments with dolphins. However, this sort of test is not quite so suitable for dolphins – they have no hands, and cannot pick off spots of paint – and it is therefore difficult to establish for certain whether they recognize themselves. When dolphins were daubed with white zinc oxide cream (the sort used on babies' bottoms), the researchers were fairly sure that they were using the mirror to examine the marks. To exclude the possibility that the animals were interacting socially with what they thought to be another dolphin, the researchers devised a rather different experiment. Instead of using a mirror, the dolphins were allowed to watch themselves on a TV screen which showed either a 'mirror image' directly relayed from a video camera or a previously recorded tape.

Dolphin Brains and Human Brains

Discussions about the relative intelligence of humans and dolphins usually centre around three measurements, which provide three different answers. Since we have very little idea about how the brains of either humans or dolphins actually work, all three are largely meaningless.

Absolute brain size is a very crude measure of mental ability. Sperm whales, with a brain weighing almost 18lb (8kg), and Asiatic elephants (16.5lb/7.5kg) have much larger brains than either dolphins (3.5lb/1.6kg for the bottlenose dolphin) or humans (3lb/1.5kg), but smart though it may be, no one is seriously suggesting that a sperm whale is five times more intelligent than a dolphin, or even a human, for that matter. Larger animals generally have larger brains.

A slightly more refined index of animal intelligence is the ratio between the size of the brain and the size of the body. Using this indicator, the bottlenose dolphin emerges with a brain body ratio less than that of humans but higher than other animals. The same result is obtained by comparing the ratio of the brain to the spinal cord.

Another favorite measurement of brain potential is the degree of folding in the surface of the brain, the argument being that these folds increase the amount of 'gray matter'. The brains of most mammals have a relatively smooth surface, while that of the human brain is extremely convoluted and the dolphin's brain even more so. This criterion is often used to contend that dolphins are more intelligent than humans.

Not all dolphins have large brains, however. Those of the river dolphins are only about half the size of those of the bottlenose dolphin. The river dolphins' echolocation abilities are broadly similar to those of the bottlenose dolphin.but they lead relatively simple social lives. Taken together, these facts suggest that the large size of most dolphin brains may have less to do with their need to interpret echolocation signals, than the result of a complex and demanding social system.

The first surprise of this experiment was that dolphins responded to the video images at all, since most animals do not respond to information presented on a TV screen. Again, the results certainly suggest that dolphins recognize themselves: some of them pulled faces and waggled their heads consistently in front of their 'mirror' image, but not when watching the playback of tapes recorded earlier.

Dolphins are not as interested in mirrors as primates, but there could be any number of reasons for this. Sight may well not be the most important sense for dolphins, and the picture they perceive in a mirror must contradict any information they receive by echolocation. Dolphins in captivity often have some experience of mirror images in the form of reflections on the glass windows in their tanks, and although windows may not be as good as a proper mirror, this does mean that seeing its own reflection is not a novelty for a dolphin in the way that it might be for a chimpanzee. Perhaps most significant of all, dolphins are more interested in each other than they are in their own reflections.

Dolphins are usually much more interested in others of their species than they are in their own reflections.

Communication and Language

Signature whistles are the dolphin's call sign and are often accompanied by a trail of bubbles. Dolphins will also call the names of others in their group – indicating a sense of 'self' and 'other'.

Taken together, these studies tell us that dolphins are large-brained animals that are probably aware of themselves as individuals. They are also capable of understanding the rudiments of a language similar to the one which humans use to communicate with each other. Whether this is a discovery that shatters the foundations of philosophy or a straightforward confirmation of what we might have expected anyway depends entirely on one's initial point of view. To explain what I mean by this, we will have to leave the subject of dolphin intelligence for a while, returning to it via a tour of French philosophy, the scientific method and chimpanzees.

Biologists have historically had a problem with animal intelligence studies which can be traced back to the seventeenth-century French philosopher René Descartes. Today historians point to Descartes as one of the most influential founders of the modern scientific method, in particular because he argued that the most productive way to think about the world was to reject 'as if absolutely false everything in which I could imagine the least doubt'.

Opposite: *In the wild, dolphins often co-ordinate their movements, which may involve partners signalling to each other. Dolphins responding to the 'Tandem Creative' command must presumably use similar signals.*

Strict adherence to this injunction has meant that scientists in general and biologists in particular have always preferred to explain the behavior of animals in terms of reflexes and genetics rather than entertain the idea that animals have a mind. This approach has been enormously successful for most of this century. It has explained very neatly how dancing bees can tell their hive-mates the direction of a rich source of food. It has given a perfectly acceptable explanation for the courtship behavior of sticklebacks and the way in which a gosling recognizes its parents. It can even resolve the question of why some animals mate with only one partner, and others with several. Only quite recently have biologists begun to observe and think about behaviors which are difficult to understand without assuming that animals have minds.

How, for instance, do you account for the sort of behavior observed by primatologist Frans de Waal and one of his students in their work on a group of captive chimpanzees at Arnhem Zoo? One of the chimps in their group, a male named Yeroen, hurt his hand in a fight with another male, Nikkie. It seemed to be troubling him, because he was limping. Frans De Waal takes up the story:

> The next day a student, Dirk Fokkema, reports that in his opinion Yeroen limps only when Nikkie is in the vicinity. I know that Dirk is a keen observer, but this time I find it hard to believe that he is correct. We go to watch and it turns out that he is indeed right: Yeroen walks past the sitting Nikkie from a point in front of him to a point behind him and the whole time Yeroen is in Nikkie's field of vision he hobbles pitifully, but once he has passed Nikkie his behavior changes and he walks normally again.
>
> (*Chimpanzee Politics*)

Whatever is going on here, it is difficult to see how it can be explained convincingly by reflexes or genetics.

It is anecdotes like this that are forcing biologists to re-evaluate the animal mind. But there is now a huge body of successful work in biology that has been accumulated thanks largely to teachers insisting that their students do not treat animals as if they had minds like humans. Among these people anthropomorphism – attributing human qualities to animals – is a very dirty word. Persuading anyone from this school of thought that 'there is not the least doubt' that animals like chimpanzees and dolphins do indeed have minds is not an easy task. They would probably argue (though perhaps without much enthusiasm) that Yeroen must have learned through previous experience that when he limped he avoided trouble with Nikkie – a simple conditioned reflex.

For many of the newer generation of biologists who are steeped in the detailed behavioral studies of chimpanzees, gorillas and the like, the product of thousands upon thousands of hours of painstaking field observations over the last thirty years or more, the results of the dolphin studies come as much less of a surprise. Dolphins, after all, are intensely social animals, and it is among the social animals, especially monkeys and apes, that intelligence has evolved on land. Many researchers are now suggesting that it may in fact be social pressure that encourages the development of intelligence in general and a sense of self in particular. The ability to imagine what another animal will do in a given situation probably allows chimpanzees to compete successfully for mates, to avoid fights and so on. And imagining what an animal is thinking and feeling inevitably must involve a mental process along the lines of 'if I were her...' The same is equally true for dolphins.

All this leaves one major question unanswered. If dolphins are intelligent, self-aware, and can understand a language similar to ours, do they have a language of their own? If the answer turns out to be yes, then many more questions automatically follow. Will we one day be able to communicate with dolphins in the way that John Lilly thought we might? Are the dolphins, as they swim through the sea, composing dolphin sagas for each other? Do they have their own history of interactions with humans, to be passed from generation to generation in some whistle-language story or sound-picture film that we cannot decipher?

One attempt to explore how dolphins might use language between themselves is a study being carried out by Diana Reiss and her co-workers at Marine

The co-ordination that dolphins use when responding to the 'Tandem Creative' command is the basis of many dolphinarium displays.

World Africa in California. They built an underwater keyboard with abstract symbols which the dolphins could press with their beaks. Each key produces a computer-generated whistle which the dolphins can hear underwater. At the same time something happens: if the dolphins press the ball symbol, a ball is thrown into the pool. The rub symbol produces a pat for the dolphin.

What this experiment has shown so far is not wildly exciting. The dolphins learn to copy the artificial whistles, and they associate these whistles with the objects subsequently placed in the pool. When playing with a ball, for example, the dolphins reproduce the ball whistle. What is interesting about this approach, however, is that it does not involve training the dolphins to perform particular human-devised tasks, but allows them to develop their own patterns of behavior – to play with the equipment in their own way. It is the sort of development that might in future allow researchers to investigate the nature of the dolphins' own vocal repertoire.

Another route for examining dolphin language may turn out to be via the study of how the animals co-ordinate their behavior. Among the 'words' understood by Phoenix and Akeakamai at the Kewalo marine laboratory are 'creative' and 'tandem'. While being trained to respond to the 'creative' command, the dolphins were given a fish every time they did something new. The concept is difficult for animals to grasp, since it seems at first as if they are just being teased – what was right yesterday is wrong today. But once they learn the rules, a spectacular sequence of

jumps, fin slaps, rolls, twists, and so on follows. 'Tandem' requires that the two dolphins perform the same action in synchrony. The interesting command is 'Tandem Creative'. An acceptable response to this might be that the dolphins swim around the tank together, leap out of the water, each doing a clockwise spin, and fall back in head first. It is the sort of display the males of a coalition might put on to impress a female they are herding. The question is, how do they do it? How do they each know what the other is planning?

One possibility is that they do not, but that one animal leads the way while the other follows so closely behind that it appears they are moving together. Dolphins are indeed incredibly good mimics, and have been seen copying the swimming patterns of seals, turtles, skates and rays, and, of course, humans. But if this sort of mimicry is really the source of the synchrony in tandem-creative performances, it is truly astounding. In a recent study, out of 467 observed tandem-creative displays, a leader could be detected by human observers in only thirty. Another possibility is that one of the dolphins can simply predict what the other is going to do as it swims around the tank at the start of its routine, but with over forty possible behavior patterns to choose from, the chances of this being feasible are remote. It is certainly conceivable that the dolphins are using sound to communicate their intentions to each other, and if so this would provide a fascinating experimental context in which to study dolphin communication.

It may be, of course, that we are looking in the wrong place altogether. Humans communicate primarily through sound, which leaves us free to look around us as we walk and talk. As speech evolved in our hominid ancestors, it may well have been important for them to concentrate their visual attention on looking out for predators. Conversely, dolphins, of course, rely largely on sound for this purpose, and to avoid being distracted might be expected to use sight as their primary means of communication.

Opposite: *In tanks and holding pens, as here at Grassy Key in Florida, dolphins almost invariably swim anti-clockwise, watching the world outside the tank through their right eye.*

Could it be that the messages passing between dolphins are chiefly visual, rather like the sign language of the deaf? It is after all the dolphins' play behavior that we take to be the equivalent of primate grooming, the social glue that keeps the society together. It would be in these close-contact bouts, as the animals touch and swim alongside each other, that a visual language might be most effective. The idea seems outlandish, but it might explain why dolphins in tanks almost always swim anti-clockwise.

Language comprehension in humans is thought to be primarily a function of the brain's left hemisphere. Separate the left hemisphere from the right by cutting through the nerve fibres that join them together (a practice occasionally carried out for medical purposes) and something odd happens. Show one of these 'split-brain' patients a shoe, and he will tell you without difficulty that he sees a shoe. Cover the right eye and show him a shoe, and he will be completely unable to name it. This is because nerves from the right eye are joined to the left-hand side of the brain, and those from the left to the right-hand side of the brain. Information from the right eye is therefore processed in the left hemisphere, the one responsible for naming. In a split-brain patient the information recorded by the right eye cannot be linked with the left hemisphere.

Dolphins face a similar problem. In a dolphin brain, the left and right hemispheres are barely connected, an evolutionary adaptation that may be associated with the way in which the animals sleep. *If* dolphins use some sort of visual language, and *if*, like humans, they use the left side of their brain to comprehend and process that language, then they might only be able to do this if they receive the information through their right eye.

People working with dolphins have known for a long time that there is something special about the right eye. Dolphins almost always swim anti-clockwise in their tanks, keeping the right eye facing outwards. They always roll over on their right side when catching fish they have driven on to a beach. Whether this relates in any way to dolphin communication is still anyone's guess, but it is an intriguing idea.

When dolphins catch fish by herding them on to a beach, they invariably roll over on to their right side. This may be connected with the way their brains interpret the world.

Whether or not dolphins actually speak to each other in ways that we might recognize as a form of language, we have established that they are intelligent animals, probably aware of themselves as individuals. If, for a moment, we leave Descartes behind, we might consider that dolphins feel emotions similar to our own. They appear to experience grief and affection in much the same way as we humans do. They can be sly and excited, mischievous and depressed. If we accept that animals like the chimpanzee and the dolphin do possess minds that are basically similar to ours, this raises some difficult questions. For Descartes, animals were machines, little different from cuckoo clocks, capable of complex

behavior but quite incapable of speech or reason. Humans were unique because they had a soul which, among other things, endowed them with the ability to speak. With this barrier between man and animals securely in place, Descartes could argue that because animals were no more than machines, they did not suffer when ill-treated and so humans were innocent 'however often they may eat or kill animals'. Take away that distinction (along with all the other fences that have been erected to separate humans from animals) and where are we? Back on the beach in the Gilbert Islands with Arthur Grimble, watching the dolphins being butchered for their meat and feeling a sense of guilt.

Dolphins in Captivity

*Performing dolphins repeat the same tricks every day, sometimes for
years. Does this lead to boredom and stress?*

The dolphin is an enigma. It is not one of the traditional collection of 'cuddly toys'
which are so influential in teaching small children to appreciate animals. It does not have
the large, soulful eyes or the other baby-like features which melt sentimental hearts. Like us
it is hairless, but the other hairless aquatic mammals, the dugong and the porpoise do not
attract the same enthusiasm, and aesthetically, most people tend to find hairless land
mammals rather revolting. Even though more and more people now spend their vacations
in places where dolphins are common, not many have ever seen a dolphin in the wild, let
alone swum with one.

Millions of us, however, have watched dolphins in captivity or on television. Much of the
interest in them that has blossomed over the last thirty years or so can be attributed to
Flipper, the dolphin who throughout the Sixties proved himself to television viewers
around the world to be every bit as smart as Lassie or Champion the Wonderhorse.

*Opposite: Captive dolphins exude a sense of playful fun, but are humans just fooled by that
fixed smile and their mastery of their element?*

*Although few bottlenose dolphins are now being taken from the wild
to stock captive displays, unusual species like these pacific white-sided
dolphins are still being captured.*

Whether framed by a TV screen or performing in front of an audience in a dolphinarium, it is at close quarters that dolphins show the characteristics we humans have come to love. With their energy, their playfulness and their apparent sense of fun, they convince us that they are happy to see us, even if we know that in truth the quizzical fixed smile is just a result of the unusual shape of the dolphin's jawline.

In both the Flipper TV shows and the theatrical surroundings of the dolphinaria, dolphins are portrayed as unfettered by the human vices of greed, malice and fear, offering us nothing less than the gift of unconditional love. Like all social animals, we are desperate to be loved, and people will travel from miles around to get their share. No one is sure of the exact figures, but it is safe to say that in the US alone more than 20 million people watch dolphins in aquaria every year.

The conditions for these captive dolphins vary enormously. In the worst, the animals may be kept in pools little bigger than themselves, and forced to repeat the same limited number of tricks for spectators day after day. These dolphins are typically bored, highly stressed and do not survive for very long. Until the late 1980s, many facilities fell into this category. In many countries, though, increasing public pressure has persuaded government agencies to introduce and enforce stringent regulations for keeping dolphins in captivity. The details vary from country to country and state to state, but typically specify a minimum depth and volume for the pools, an appropriate sex ratio, minimal standards of healthcare and an associated program of public education. In the USA, at least, dolphinaria are obliged by law to educate their visitors. Some of the educational programs are both extensive and excellent. The Monterey Bay Aquarium in California, for example, devotes fifty staff members, 600 volunteers and about $2 million (£1.3 million) a year to education. But not all dolphinaria share this attitude, and in some such programs are given only the minimal resources needed to meet the legal requirements.

Increasingly, the terms of licences also stipulate that no healthy animals are to be taken from the wild in order to stock the facilities. In several dolphinaria the majority of the animals now on display have either been bred in captivity or rescued after beaching or accidents. It appears that, in the case of bottlenose dolphins at least, no animals at all have been captured from the wild to stock facilities in the USA throughout the 1990s, thanks largely to improved husbandry techniques and increased experience with managing captive animals. In fact, the main problems now centre around how to release surplus captive animals back into the wild.

Dolphins that have been taken into captivity probably now have a life expectancy similar to what it would be in the wild. It is very difficult to be precise about this, because the life-expectancy figures for both captive and wild animals are inadequate, and the dangers are significantly different. In the wild, many dolphins die within the first six months of birth, falling prey to sharks or other predators. In captivity, on the other hand, sharks are not usually a threat, and both the birth rate and calf survival are probably actually higher. However, the overall mortality is still greater than the overall birth rate, and the captive population is still declining. In the highly charged atmosphere of the debate, both sides are tempted to cook the figures, which must be read very carefully. For example, one recent report argued: 'On average the expected lifespan of a bottlenose dolphin in captivity could be as little as fourteen years, while in the wild the dolphin could live twenty to twenty-nine years.' As a human, I could live to be 110, but my average expected lifespan is only about seventy years, whether I spend it in the wild or in captivity.

If dolphins are to be kept in captivity it is important that they receive plenty of mental stimulation. In the wild they would spend much of their time foraging for food, and so training helps to redirect their attention and give them something else to think about. It is also important in helping veterinarians look after the animals properly: dolphins can be trained to co-operate with medical examinations, allowing their carers to take blood or run ultrasound scans. Dolphins can even be taught to give a urine sample by peeing into a bottle.

It would seem that captivity does not have profound ill effects on dolphins, especially in those facilities where they are regularly trained to perform complex and demanding manoeuvres, as in the traditional dolphin displays. Nevertheless, dolphins are, as we know, intelligent, social animals, and there is certainly evidence that they do not positively enjoy it. Captive dolphins have often developed gastro-intestinal ulcers, a complaint usually associated with stress in humans, and postmortem examination often shows them to have enlarged adrenal glands, again, generally taken to be a sign of stress. To some extent, the response of dolphins to captivity is beyond their captors' control, and depends on the individual animal. One pilot whale apparently adapted well but became depressed following the death of his mate. After four years of treatment, including anti-depressant drugs and tranquillizers, he was eventually rehabilitated and released back into the wild.

Indications of stress in captivity can be even more dramatic. On at least two separate occasions dolphins have been seen to swim at full speed into the walls of their tanks. Both knocked themselves unconscious and subsequently died. Richard O'Barry, trainer of five of the dolphins that collectively played Flipper, believes that one of his charges, too, committed suicide. When the series ended, Kathy was retired to a small steel tank, where she was denied the same level of contact with either people or other dolphins. O'Barry is convinced that she became lonely and depressed and decided to die. 'It was deliberate,' he says. 'Every breath is a conscious effort for a dolphin, and she just stopped breathing. She died of a broken heart.'

A killer whale stands on its tail to 'kiss' its trainer and so demonstrate its complete subservience to man.

Seen from an evolutionary perspective, humans are simply one species among many struggling to survive and reproduce, with no claim to superiority. So what justification can we possibly have for imprisoning any of our fellow creatures, let alone animals that might well be aware of what is happening to them? For Ric O'Barry, and others like him, the answer is none. Since resigning from his job as a dolphin trainer, O'Barry has spent his time campaigning against the captivity of dolphins and helping to rehabilitate captives for release back into the wild. He has been arrested many times for his activities, which have included attempts to rescue dolphins from aquaria without first asking the owners' permission.

The issue stirs enormously powerful emotions in anyone who has been involved with these playful, lovable animals. It is difficult to remain dispassionate. Few who care about either animals or the environment

would argue with the premise that since captivity causes dolphins stress and suffering, and since they are, it seems, conscious and self-aware, then we ought not keep them in tanks. No one would deny that we must find ways to stop the annual slaughter of half a million dolphins worldwide with fishing nets and pollution. The question is, can we raise public concern sufficiently to halt the killing without keeping animals on public display? Would Richard O'Barry have become such a committed campaigner were it not for his early experience with Flipper?

Whether humans have grounds for inflicting captivity on dolphins depends on your point of view, and that may be influenced by the benefits to both people and dolphins as a result. If captive dolphins can help to educate people about the plight of their wild cousins, then perhaps the end justifies the means?

The contention is that the better the educational material, the posters and the classes provided around the dolphin exhibit, the easier it is to justify the retention of wild animals in captivity. In a sense, though, these peripheral materials are a separate issue. It would be perfectly possible to hold classes on dolphin physiology or ecology without a captive dolphin, and many universities around the world do it all the time. The most relevant question is what visitors actually learn about dolphins by watching the exhibitions. As Umberto Eco, journalist, author and professor of semiotics at the University of Bologna in Italy, has observed, the lessons of the show itself are subtle, and may in fact contradict the educational material. He chose to illustrate the point with a story about captive orcas, but a similar argument could be made for any dolphin display:

In the marine amphitheatre where the trained whales perform, these animals are billed as 'killer whales,' and probably they are very dangerous when they're hungry. Once we are convinced that they are dangerous, it is very satisfying to see them so obedient to orders, diving, racing, leaping into the air, until they actually snatch the fish from the trainer's hand and reply with almost human moans to the questions they are asked. *(Travels in Hyperreality)*

Killer whales perform in the theatrical surroundings of
Sea World, San Diego.

Shows like this apparently affirm our power as humans over the animal world. But while many of the tricks are taken from the old circus repertoire, and include forcing the animals to leap through burning hoops, or to lie docile while the trainer sticks his head into their gaping mouths – the 'taming' of the orcas does not follow quite the same pattern as the circus act with the lions and the lion-tamer. There is no whip, no chair to keep the animals at bay, no sign of resistance from the dolphins. As Eco argues, the underlying message of the dolphin display is not just that man can dominate nature; it is the projection of a golden age in which the struggle for survival between man and animals has ceased to exist and co-operation has replaced conflict. In this vision humans are still superior to dolphins in every way, but if the dolphins accept their place in the hierarchy, then we can work together.

So one facet of the dolphin show is the ritual enactment of a modern myth – except that, unlike the Greek dolphin myths, it is a carefully constructed lie. While the Greek myths were the expression of unobservable truths in terms of observable realities, the dolphin display is a dangerous fantasy. The animals learn their tricks as the result of many hours of coaching, but in the theatrical context of the performance, this training is concealed to encourage the illusion. As Eco puts it:

The tricks performed by dolphins are often old circus tricks, but the relationship between dolphin and trainer is portrayed as being achieved through co-operation rather than coercion.

The killer whales perform a square dance and answer the trainer's questions not because they have acquired linguistic ability, but because they have been trained through conditioned reflexes, and we interpret the stimulus response relationship as a relationship of meaning.

It is the shattering of a similar golden-age myth that made Arthur Grimble feel so uncomfortable as he stood on the beach in Kiribati.

My mind still shrinks from that last scene – the raving humans, the beasts so triumphantly at rest.

Grimble found himself on a beautiful tropical island, and his romantic temperament got the better of him. It came as something of a shock to realize that the islanders who lived 'in harmony' with dolphins also ate them. Not only that, they enjoyed it.

Like most people who really do live 'close to nature', the dolphin-callers of Kiribati knew in a sense that we have long forgotten that their very existence depended on the natural world around them. They were an integral part of that world. Not above it in any way, not at the pinnacle of creation, but simply a part of the great web of life. They would also have understood the importance of maintaining the fabric of that web to ensure their own survival.

Meeting Dolphins for Ourselves

Funghie, known to some as Dorad, the bottlenose dolphin who chose to socialize with humans in Dingle Bay, Ireland.

Performing dolphins may give us confusing messages about our place in nature, and our relationship to it, but such displays, of course, are not the only way to see dolphins. Growing numbers of people prefer the idea of swimming with them, being involved with the animal in some way rather than passively sitting and watching a theatrical production. No doubt swimming with a dolphin can create an illusion of harmony between man and animal, but it is likely to be tempered by the often very immediate knowledge that the seas are not very clean, and that the dolphin is an animal in its own right. The exact implications of this sort of interaction for the people involved, for the dolphins and for conservation depend on whether the dolphins are captive or wild and on how well the interaction is managed by whoever is responsible for bringing people and dolphins together.

Opposite: *Swimming with a dolphin may create an illusion of harmony between human and animal, at least for humans.*

The effect of being in the water with a dolphin can be enormously powerful – so powerful, in fact, that the practice has been suggested as a treatment for disorders that are difficult for conventional medicine to tackle. It is claimed that people with social and emotional problems like depression, anorexia and autism respond well to what has become known as 'dolphin therapy'. The prospect of vulnerable people who are seriously ill being encouraged to spend what could be quite sizeable amounts of money in search of a cure should make anyone exploring such promises extremely cautious. On the other hand, if there is a chance that the claims are true, they should be taken seriously, especially when other treatments have failed.

Anorexia and autism are, as far as we can tell, uniquely human illnesses, and at first sight jumping into the sea with a large marine mammal is not a likely way to cure them. But many people who have previously suffered years of anxiety and despair certainly feel that they have been helped by the experience. English teenager Jemima Biggs had been clinically depressed since the age of nine, and following the death of a close friend and the failure of a relationship she became anorexic at sixteen. When she was seventeen she met Dorad, the 'friendly' dolphin of Ireland's Dingle Bay. She is not clear herself how this encounter affected her, although she is quite convinced that it represented a turning point in her life. One aspect of the encounter that seems to have been important to Jemima was simply that Dorad chose to swim with her.

At a time in your life when you're feeling utterly despicable, the dolphin is actually choosing to be with you. He doesn't demand anything from you, you have nothing to prove. I could not do anything impressive to warrant his attention, yet there was something about me which was apparently worth his time. My sense of self-esteem was so low that to suddenly feel so special, and especially without doing anything to earn it, was a poignant and very powerful moment.

(*BBC Wildlife Magazine*, September 1991)

Just as there are people around who choose to believe that dolphins are ambassadors from Sirius, or that they are in telepathic communication with selected humans, there is no shortage of proponents of the view that the animals can heal through their own conscious will, using their sonar system in some way to diagnose and readjust our human energies. There is nothing in Jemima Biggs' story, or in any of the other accounts of therapeutic encounters with dolphins, that provides evidence for this. Other animals are known to have similar effects. Dogs and cats are now frequently used in hospitals to help anxious patients to relax, often with spectacular results. Any benefits that people gain by swimming with dolphins are likely of the same order, and entirely in the mind of the patient – though no less real and important for that, of course.

Until quite recently, the only way to swim with a dolphin was to visit one of the sociable creatures like Dorad, which, over the centuries have chosen, for reasons best known to themselves, to seek the companionship of humans. These animals, usually solitary male bottlenose dolphins, are in some ways the ideal for this purpose. Since they have chosen to seek human company in the open sea, there are no concerns over the ethics of keeping wild animals in captivity, and there are fewer worries about stressing a wild animal by forcing it into close proximity with people. But as we saw in the opening section, these solitary dolphins can be mischievous, and even dangerous. They are also rather rare animals, and with so many people wanting their half-hour of fun in the water, there are just nowhere near enough Dorads, Tiaos and Opos to go round.

Consequently, many 'eco-tour' operators have come up with alternatives to give their clients a chance to see dolphins in their natural surroundings, warts and all. Unless the dolphins are attracted with bait (a practice now outlawed in the US and New Zealand because of the associated risks to dolphins from rancid food, boat propellers and sharks), the

Opposite: *For tourists, swimming with dolphins can be the experience of a lifetime, but it can sometimes be stressful for the dolphins.*

Above: *This is the ideal of eco-tourism – the chance to watch whales in a beautiful and uncluttered environment without causing stress to the animals.*

Right: *A well-made documentary can be entertaining as well as informative.*

animals may choose not to turn up at all. If they do put in an appearance they may spend only a very short time near the tourists. Yet even so such visits may be useful in educating the holidaymakers. They will travel to and from the meeting point; they will witness at first hand the boats, the jet-skis, the pollution, and anything else that might threaten the survival of the animals they have come to see. They will have the opportunity to leave as well-informed ambassadors for the conservation of dolphins.

The eco-tourism industry promises many things. To the tourist it offers the chance to see wild animals in their natural state; to the conservationist it holds out the hope of stemming the tide of environmental destruction. By effectively increasing the financial value of the natural resources concerned, eco-tourism encourages their protection by local people. And to the tour operators, it offers the prospect of increased profits.

As long as tourists are prepared to pay handsomely for the privilege of seeing dolphins (and plenty are), this seems on the surface to be a magical formula

from which everyone benefits. Yet there are dangers which the growing popularity of such tours will increase. The irony is that concerned, eco-friendly visitors may themselves form part of the problem. While the eco-tourism industry claims to respect the environments in which it works, this is easier said than done, especially as the pressure of numbers builds. Boats and snorkellers stir up sediments, and in the long term this can damage coral reefs. A tour operator might be able to run one trip daily to a dolphin school, and the animals might be inquisitive enough to visit the boat of their own accord and even get accustomed to swimmers in the water. But what happens when there are two boats, or three, or five, and after the first few visits the dolphins get bored and swim off to rest or feed? What happens when the dolphins are ill, or socializing with other dolphins, or are involved in courtship?

Inevitably, there is a risk that instead of contact being made at the dolphins' choosing, the animals will be followed and harassed by tour operators eager to satisfy their customers. There is no question that many eco-tour companies are truly committed to conserving the animals and environments they visit, but without very careful monitoring of the industry they are likely to be put out of business by less scrupulous competitors. In many of the most popular whale- and dolphin-watching areas, alarm bells are already being sounded.

An additional worry must be that eco-tourism is for the vast majority of people simply not an affordable option. Visiting a school of free-swimming dolphins in their natural habitat in small, closely supervised groups may meet the requirements of both dolphins and tourists in the short term, but if this is the only remaining way to see the dolphins at close quarters in the next century, then there is a danger that most people will lose interest in their plight.

It is often argued that television can fill this gap, allowing a vast global audience to experience nature without leaving their sitting rooms. In reality, though, even factual, well-made TV documentaries do not turn armchair tourists into committed campaigners for conservation. At best they might encourage people to go and look for themselves, and take the

first step on what might be the path to real involvement. At worst, they can, like dolphinaria, purvey the golden-age myth. Everything within the TV screen is peace, harmony, and totally natural – just don't ask about the bits you can't see.

At this point it is almost impossible to escape a feeling that doom is closing in all around. TV rarely generates commitment; eco-tourism is too restricted in its availability to influence the majority; dolphinaria send out the wrong messages. Is there any way out?

One possibility might be a relatively new approach now being adopted by several aquaria in Florida and Hawaii. In return for between $50 and $100 (£35–£67), members of the public can spend, say, up to an hour swimming with captive dolphins. Although there is no doubt that for the humans involved, this can be the 'experience of a lifetime', for the dolphins, on the other hand, it may mean repeated periods of stress, especially if there is no 'safe haven' to which they can retreat.

Giving humans the opportunity to swim with dolphins in captivity fulfils many needs. It allows large numbers of people access to the experience and the chance to engage their emotions in a way that can be life-transforming. Although the captive-swim programs often involve trained dolphins performing 'tricks' for the clients in a manner reminiscent of the trained animals of the dolphin shows, the more informal, less theatrical setting makes these seem of less symbolic relevance. Most importantly, after such an experience, most people are probably prepared to take the time to check that the tuna tin they take from the supermarket shelf is labelled 'dolphin-friendly'. For a few, it might even be the moment that triggers a lifelong commitment to working to protect the animals and their environment. Captive-swim programs do take some of the pressure off the dolphins' natural habitat, and they do not promulgate the insidious myth of a golden age. Whether or not they are an acceptable solution to the problem of promoting dolphin conservation depends on which side one takes on the thorny issue of keeping dolphins in captivity.

Looking further into the future, several different organizations are presently exploring the possibility of using technology to create the illusion of an encounter.

Swimming With Dolphins: A Code of Conduct

The following code of conduct has been drawn up by International Dolphin Watch, a non-profit organization supporting dolphin conservation.

Boat Users

Do not chase dolphins or drive a boat directly towards them. Wherever possible, let them approach you.

Do not make sudden bursts of speed or violent changes of direction; dolphins may be out of sight under your boat.

Do not stop or slow down suddenly. This can confuse and alarm dolphins as much as sudden acceleration.

Users of twin screw boats, do not manoeuvre using the screws in opposition, as this creates violent and confusing water movements.

Do ensure that no more than one boat is within 328ft (100m) or three boats within 0.6 miles (1km) of dolphins at any one time.

Swimmers

Until a close relationship has been established, it is important that swimmers do not attempt to touch the dolphins. Let them take the initiative.

Wear a buoyancy aid and do not wear or carry sharp objects that could damage a dolphin's skin.

Do not harass a dolphin when it is feeding.

Do not attempt to feed wild dolphins. This is illegal in many countries, attracts sharks, can poison the dolphins, and can encourage the dolphins to take fishing bait which can result in serious injury.

Do not try to manipulate the dolphins – they are not there to perform.

Do not stray too far from the boat or land.

Do not go into the water in large numbers and crowd the dolphins.

Never, Ever chase a dolphin. Let them approach you.

Do not touch a dolphin on the head, especially around the animal's blow-hole or in the area around its eyes and ears.

Fishermen

Do not cast lines or leave them set when there are dolphins close by.

Finally

Do take care of the environment as well as the dolphins. Remove all rubbish to appropriate disposal sites.

Do not collect or buy plants taken from the wild, coral or other wildlife souvenirs.

Do treat local people with respect, especially when visiting dolphins in the majority world. Facilities may be basic and things will almost certainly not happen how, or when you expect them to. Remember that if dolphin-watching is a positive experience for the local community, this is the best protection the dolphins can have. Be tolerant.

The approaches being examined at the moment range from the relatively straightforward use of recorded dolphin sounds played back over a conventional tape-recorder to the cutting edge of computer simulation technology. Using virtual reality techniques, groups in the US and Japan are investigating ways in which every aspect of the interaction between humans and dolphins could be simulated. In a few years' time, this technology or something similar might provide an alternative and less harmful way for people to 'meet' dolphins. Whether this sort of simulated interaction between people and animals will encourage respect for the natural world, or simply become another game in the world's computer arcades, remains to be seen. Electronic gadgetry can help to educate, to inform, and to entertain. But most people who are involved in conservation work would point to some interaction with a real live animal, or at least a living environment, as the trigger that set them on their course. Perhaps virtual reality will one day have its uses, but for the moment the acrimonious debate over captive dolphins looks set to rumble on.

The Survival of the Species

A spotted dolphin female with her calf. Wild dolphins have a secure future only if we humans stop polluting the oceans and entangling them in fishing nets.

From the ancient myths about dolphins, passed by word of mouth, to the prospect of swimming with dolphins in a computer-simulated virtual-reality world, it seems we have come a long way. We no longer believe that dolphins carry us to our final resting place on the Isles of the Blest, and we know a great deal more about their lives. But while we continue to convince ourselves, even subconsciously, that we share some mystic bond with these animals, we risk turning them into the victims of our dreams.

The golden age of peaceful co-existence between man and the natural world which is the central message of the dolphin shows has in reality never been more remote. We are, at the moment, witnessing perhaps the most devastating wave of extinctions our planet has ever experienced.

Opposite: *Today, we tend to reinterpret the dolphin-rider myths. We like to persuade ourselves that harmony between humans and dolphins is a present reality. It has never been more remote.*

Above: *In many parts of the world, dolphins are still being killed for food, or shark bait.*
(Page 146–147): *Poisons ingested by the female dolphins are stored in the blubber and subsequently
passed to their offspring with the milk.*

The loss of plant and animal species is already on the same scale as the mass extinction that brought about the demise of the dinosaurs. Perhaps as many as half the species that lived on earth 10,000 years ago have already gone forever. There is every chance that we humans will join them, becoming unable to survive in the world we are making. We may last the next fifty years, or even the next 1,000, but on the evolutionary time scale 1,000 years is less than the blink of an eye. Part of the appeal of the dolphin displays is that their subliminal messages of hope, optimism and harmony between man and the natural world deny this appalling reality.

As one of the oceans' top predators, dolphins are sensitive to quite small changes in water quality. Poisonous chemicals washed into the sea in low concentrations may not affect plankton or fish themselves. However, because dolphins are ingesting large quantities of fish every day, many of these chemicals are concentrated in their bodies and they grow sick. Their state of health indicates the health of the oceans, alerting us to changes in water quality of which we might otherwise be unaware.

Over the last few years, the warnings have been coming thick and fast. In the summer of 1987 hundreds of bottlenose dolphins were washed up along the coast of New Jersey and the eastern United States. In 1989, hundreds more died along the north eastern coast of France. On three separate occasions in the early 1990s, large numbers of bottlenose dolphins were found dead in the Gulf of Mexico and this also happened with striped dolphins in the Mediterranean.

Tuna Fishing and Dolphins

In a vast area of the ocean stretching from Mexico to Chile, schools of large yellowfin tuna swim with schools of spotted and spinner dolphins. Exactly why these animals stay together remains unclear, although for much of this century fishermen have taken advantage of the association, using the dolphins as a way of locating the tuna. Until the 1960s, the tuna were caught with rod and line, but as the fishing became more commercialized large vessels began to net them — with disastrous results for the dolphins.

The first step in setting a net for a shoal of tuna is to find the dolphins that travel with them. Once a suitable shoal has been located, a small boat takes one end of the seine net, while the mother ship races to encircle the tuna, and the dolphins along with them. The net is then pulled beneath the animals, to create a 'purse', from which there is no escape. In theory, the dolphins could quite easily leap over the cork line of the net and escape to freedom, but for some reason they do not. Perhaps they fear what might be on the other side. As a result, by the end of the 1960s an estimated quarter of a million dolphins were dying in the nets of the US tuna fleet every year.

When biologists and the public learned the scale of the destruction in the tuna-fishing industry, there was an outcry that has led to a substantial reduction in the losses. Fishermen and biologists have developed a variety of techniques to avoid capturing the dolphins, which include backing the mother ship into the pursed net so that the trailing edge of the net drops below the waterline, allowing the dolphins to stream out. Laws were passed restricting the number of dolphins it was acceptable for the US fleet to catch along with the tuna, but since these laws had no power over non-US fleets, they had a limited effect. The greatest breakthrough came as the result of the actions of ordinary people, who simply refused to buy tuna whose capture harmed dolphins, and so forced the fishermen of all nations to adopt a more responsible attitude.

The campaign involved simply labelling cans of tuna for sale in supermarkets as 'dolphin-safe' or 'dolphin-friendly'. There are several criteria which qualify manufacturers to use this claim in their packaging. An official observer must certify that dolphins were not intentionally circled as the net was set, or the tuna must be caught outside the Eastern Tropical Pacific, or the boat used must be small, or a technique other than purse seining must be employed. Even more stringent are the requirements of the 'Flipper Seal of Approval' program. To earn the right to display this label, a company must also donate money to help with monitoring and inspection.

The situation has improved dramatically since the 1960s, thanks largely to consumer pressure. Unfortunately, though, many thousand dolphins do still die in fishing nets every year, and it is crucial that conservationists maintain the pressure on tuna fisheries, in particular, to ensure that all tuna labelled as dolphin-friendly is indeed safely caught.

Just one of thousands. A pacific white-sided dolphin drowned after being entangled in a Japanese drift net in the North Pacific.

Releasing Captives into the Wild

When zoos first began to build their collections back in the nineteenth century, they were already more than just a menagerie of captive animals: they symbolized the conquest of distant lands, the self-evident superiority of the Empire over its subject peoples, and, of course, their wildlife. An explorer would send home a tiger or an elephant as a patriotic gesture, while subject nations would donate wild animals to the zoos of their conquerors as tribute.

Visitors were at first happy to stroll through the grounds viewing the caged animals like paintings in an art gallery and bathing in the reflected glory of their Empire. But the novelty soon wore off, and zoos began to search for new ways to attract customers. Foremost among these was the zoos' claim to further public knowledge and

Releasing a small porpoise that has been trapped in a fishing net is not too difficult. Releasing a fully-grown killer whale that has lived its entire life in an aquarium is a different matter.

enlightenment, and more recently many zoos have taken on what many biologists would agree is an important role in the captive breeding and conservation of endangered species.

Dolphinaria justify taking dolphins into captivity by the rather older claim that their displays increase public awareness of the animal and its problems in the wild, and so encourage its protection. Although several dolphinaria can point to successful births in captivity as evidence that the animals in their charge are reasonably healthy, they cannot claim that their captive breeding directly contributes to the wild dolphin population, or is ever likely to do so.

Only the Yangzi dolphin is at present so critically endangered in the wild that captive breeding can possibly have any significant effect on the total population. Ironically, the best chance for the medium-term survival of this species probably does depend on breeding in a captive or semi-captive situation, but there are no Yangzi dolphins in captivity outside China, and only one there. The local government in Auhui province recently offered a reward of over $10,000 US dollars for every dolphin captured and taken alive to their breeding and protection facility on the Yangzi river. If the Yangzi dolphin is ever bred successfully, it will be largely due to the experience gained with bottlenose and other dolphins which have been kept primarily for display purposes.

During the last few years, tougher regulations on keeping dolphins in captivity have forced many dolphinaria to close. At the same time, the reduction in the conflict between the superpowers and the consequent cutbacks in defence spending have resulted in several dolphins previously involved in naval research being declared 'surplus to navy requirements'. These animals were being trained to retrieve lost missiles from the sea bed, and, according to some reports, were being equipped with compressed-air guns with which they would kill enemy divers. As with most military operations, there is a good deal about military dolphin research that we do not know, and no doubt much of what we have been told is nonsense.

Whatever their backgrounds, releasing these animals back into the wild is no simple matter. A dolphin used to captivity obviously has problems readjusting to life in the sea, and without the protection of a school, it will probably soon be eaten by sharks, even if it can remember enough about the world outside its tank to find its own food. Ideally the animal should be freed close to the school from which it was taken. Not only is there a chance that the captive might have some memory of the animals with which it once swam, but perhaps more importantly, this practice minimizes the risk of introducing inherited diseases into a different wild population previously free of them. A separate but equally vital consideration is the danger of introducing contagious diseases contracted in captivity into the wild, and it is obviously crucial that the health of the dolphin is carefully monitored before it is released.

Only with what can be a very long process of rehabilitation, and more than a little luck, is it possible to return captive dolphins to their natural habitat — and at an estimated cost per dolphin of anywhere between $12,000 and $75,000(£8,000–£50,000), rehabilitation is very expensive. Costs for releasing captive killer whales are even higher. Something close to $5 million (£3.3 million) has been raised for the liberty of Keiko, the captive killer whale who starred in the Warner Bros movie Free Willy. In the film, Willy is returned to the wild, but for the real Willy the road to freedom is proving long, hard and controversial. Not only is it doubtful that Keiko can ever be released successfully after twelve years in captivity, but many people question the wisdom of spending so much on a single animal when the money might in theory be used to improve our knowledge and ability to protect those animals that remain in the wild. Conversely, supporters of the campaign to free the real Willy argue that a gesture like this sends vital messages about the rights of animals and the limits on the rights of humans to exploit them.

Unless captive animals can be successfully replaced in their natural environment, this debate is rather pointless. So far, the results of attempts to do so have been mixed. At one end of the spectrum are animals like the male bottlenose dolphin Flipper, who was released in southern Brazil in 1993 after approximately ten years in captivity. Flipper's is a success story, and he has been seen repeatedly since his release, often in the company of other dolphins, apparently behaving perfectly normally. Others, like Rajah, who was returned to a group of dolphins off the coast of Perth, Western Australia after eleven years, have not fared so well. At first, Rajah appeared to mix naturally with wild bottlenose dolphins, but eleven days later he followed the research vessel that had accompanied him on his release back into harbour. When he was recaptured he was found to have lost 40lb (18kg), a little more than a tenth of his body weight.

Previous page: *Images of dolphins that we find attractive perhaps reflect our longing to share what appears to be a peaceful, untroubled world.*

Right: *Short-finned pilot whales.*

Another major incident involving the deaths of several hundred dolphins, occurred in the Gulf of California in early 1995. As the campaigning environmental organization Greenpeace puts it, taken together these cases are 'a tragic symbol of a decaying coastal ecosystem'.

Apart from the recent incident in the Gulf of California, which was the result of toxic marker dyes being used by drug smugglers, most if not all of these deaths have occurred as a result of infection with a newly discovered virus – one of the group of viruses known as a *morbillivirus*. Related to the canine distemper virus, this class can cause pneumonia and brain damage. What is frightening about the deaths is that the virus does not work alone. The evidence suggests that although the disease caused by the virus is directly responsible for most of the deaths, the epidemics are spreading quickly through the dolphin population because the dolphins' immune system has been weakened by poisons that have accumulated in their fatty tissues, livers and kidneys.

The chemicals responsible are members of the notorious family of organochlorine pesticides, including DDT, PCBs, dioxin and chlordane. Although many countries have banned the use of these pesticides, insecticides applied years ago are still finding their way from the land to the sea. These are then concentrated in the marine food chain and end up in the bodies of dolphins. In males, the concentration of organochlorines may be great enough to impair the production of testosterone, and so to interfere with the animal's reproductive ability. Females are not affected in the same way, but in their case the consequences are perhaps even more worrying: 80 per cent of the DDT and PCB contaminants in a mother's blubber are transferred to her firstborn calf, further concentrating the toxins from generation to generation. In the blubber of most of the dead dolphins recovered from the east coast of the USA in 1987, the concentration of PCBs was so high that to meet American health and safety legislation the bodies should have been treated as toxic waste when the time came to dispose of their remains.

It is in handling this sort of problem that we humans desperately need our mythology and our symbols. We carry on treating the sea as a dumping ground because at the moment another myth is dominant in our culture: the myth of industrial progress. So prevalent is this idea that most of us in the consumptive world take it to be an inevitability, while for the majority world it is largely irrelevant.

It might seem that the destruction of our coastal ecosystems needs no mythic explanation since it is itself an observable truth. But the concept of progress is so powerful that it blinds us to reality. We are, after all, animals; our evolution and culture have equipped

us to think only of our own survival, and that of our children. We seem incapable of looking beyond that and considering the long-term consequences of our actions. We can easily understand that if we continue to treat the oceans as a global rubbish pit, we will end up poisoning ourselves, but we seem powerless to think of ways to stop this happening.

The dolphins are another life form, wonderful and strange, but they depend on us. We are no better than dolphins, but we do have the power to destroy them. And we cannot escape the responsibility that power gives us simply by swimming with dolphins, or by longing to share their apparently untroubled world. If dolphins are not to become the victims of our self-deluding golden-age dreams, we must think less about how we can use them to cure our own ills and concentrate instead on how we can halt their destruc-

tion and undo the damage we have already done to them.

Perhaps the dolphins can help us in this. If they have a symbolic value today it is as a symbol of a clean and healthy environment. Foul up the seas and the dolphins will be among the first to go. As such a symbol, they might help us realize that our image of these marvelous, intelligent, sentient creatures swimming free in boundless, crystal-clear waters is a goal, not a fact. Measure progress by how closely we approach that goal and we might ourselves survive to see it achieved. It will be many years before we can develop the tools to discover what dolphins think, to unravel the detail of how they communicate. If we do not act now to help ensure their survival, they may not be around to ask when the time comes. And for that matter, neither may we.

Selected Bibliography

Bryden, Dr M.M., and Sir Richard Harrison, (consultant eds.), *Whales, Dolphins and Porpoises,* Merehurst Press, London, 1988.

Conner, Richard C. and Micklethwaite Peterson, Dawn, *The Lives of Whales and Dolphins,* Henry Holt and Co., New York, 1994.

Donoghue, Michael and Wheeler, Annie, *Dolphins, Their Life and Survival,* Blandford Press, Auckland, 1990.

Eco, Umberto, *Travels in Hyperreality,* Picador, 1987. First published in the UK by Secker & Warburg Ltd under the title *Faith in Fakes,* 1986. (Excerpts from *Travels in Hyperreality* by Umberto Eco, translated by William Weaver, copyright © 1983, 1976, 1973 by Gruppo Editoriale Fabgri-Bompiani, Sonzogno, Etas S.p.A., English translation copyright © 1986 by Harcourt Brace & Company, reprinted by permission of Harcourt Brace & Company.)

Hoyt, Erich, *Riding with Dolphins – The Equinox Guide to Dolphins and Porpoises,* Camden House, Ontario, 1992.

Lilly, John C., *Man and Dolphin,* Victor Gollancz, London, 1962.

May, John (ed.), *The Greenpeace Book of Dolphins,* Sterling Publishing Co, New York, 1990.

Norris, Kenneth S., *Dolphin Days,* published in the USA by W.W. Norton and Co., New York, 1991, and in the UK by John Murray (Publishers) Ltd, 1991.

Pliny the Elder, *Natural History: A Selection by Pliny the Elder,* translated by John F. Healy, (Penguin Classics) London, 1991. (Quotation on page 72 reproduced by permission of Penguin Books Ltd).

Pryor, Karen and Norris, Kenneth S., *Dolphin Societies, Discoveries and Puzzles,* University of California Press, 1991.

Rabinovitch, Melitta, *The Dolphin in Greek Legend and Myth,* translated by Richard M. Brown from *Der Dolphin in Sage und Mythos der Greichen* (Dornach: Hyberniq-Verlag, 1947), in *Alexandria, the Journal of Western Cosmological Traditions,* 2, Phanes Press, 1993, ed. David Fideler.

Slater, Candace, *Dance of the Dolphin: Transformation and Disenchantment in the Amazonian Imagination,* University of California Press, 1994.

de Waal, Frans, *Chimpanzee Politics,* in Byrne, R. and Whiten, A., *Machiavellian Intelligence,* Clarendon Press, 1988.

Appendix:

Classification of dolphins

Given the uncertainty of relationships between dolphins, the following list makes no attempt to group them into families or subfamilies beyond the relatively straightforward distinction between the river dolphins and the marine dolphins. The list also includes two species where some authorities recognize only one. This has been done to make the list more useful to anyone trying to link common and Latin names, and does not imply agreement with any particular system.

The River Dolphins
Superfamily *Platanistoidea*

Platanista gangetica	Ganges river dolphin or susu
Platanista minor	Indus river dolphin or susu
Lipotes vexillifer	Baiji, or Yangzi river dolphin
Pontoporia blainvillei	Franciscana, or La Plata dolphin
Inia geoffrensis	Amazon river dolphin, or boto

The Marine Dolphins
Family *Delphinidae*

Steno bredanensis	Rough-toothed dolphin
Sousa chinensis	Indopacific hump-backed dolphin
Suusa teuszii	Atlantic hump-backed dolphin
Sotalia fluviatilis	Tucuxi
Lagenorhynchus albirostris	White-beaked dolphin
Lagenorhynchus acutus	Atlantic white-sided dolphin
Lagenorhynchus obscurus	Dusky dolphin
Lagenorhynchus obliquidens	Pacific white-sided dolphin
Lagenorhynchus cruciger	Hourglass dolphin
Lagenorhynchus australis	Peale's dolphin
Grampus griseus	Risso's dolphin
Tursiops truncatus	Bottlenose dolphin
Stenella frontalis	Atlantic spotted dolphin
Stenella attenuata	Pantropical spotted dolphin
Stenella longirostris	Spinner dolphin
Stenella clymene	Clymene dolphin
Stenella coeruleoalba	Striped dolphin
Delphinus delphis	Common dolphin
Delphinus capensis	William Dall's dolphin
Lagenodelphis hosei	Fraser's dolphin
Lissodelphis borealis	Northern right whale dolphin
Lissodelphis peronii	Southern right whale dolphin
Orcaella brevirostris	Irrawaddy dolphin, pesut
Cephalorhynchus commersonii	Commerson's dolphin
Cephalorhynchus eutropis	Black or Chilean dolphin
Cephalorhynchus hectori	Heaviside's dolphin
Cephalorhynchus heavisidii	Hector's dolphin
Peponocephala electra	Melon-headed whale, or electra dolphin
Feresa attenuata	Pygmy killer whale
Pseudorca crassidens	False killer whale
Orcinus orca	Orca or killer whale
Globicephala melas	Long-finned pilot whale
Globicephala macrorhynchus	Short-finned pilot whale

Index

(Numbers in italics refer to illustrations)

Picture Acknowledgments

Ancient Art and Architecture Collection: 10, 11; 142 (B. Wilson)

Ardea London Limited: 58-59 (Jean-Paul Ferrero); 41, 102-103, 113, 132-133 (Kenneth W. Fink); 16, 32 (Andrea Florence); 8, 15 top left, 22-23, 38, 46, 52-53, 62, 63, 70-71, 73, 79, 84-85, 86, 95, 100-101, 118, 137, 148, 150-151 (Francois Gohier); 98, 104, 105, 111, 117 (Denise Herzing); 106-107 (David D. Parker); 65 top left and top right (D. Parer & E. Parer-Cook); 26 (Ron & Valerie Taylor)

Bruce Coleman Limited: 122 (Altante SDF); 45, 54-55 (Ken Balcomb); 68-69 (Jen & Des Bartlett); 115 (John Cancalosi); 18 (Neville Coleman); 33 top right (Alain Compost); 34-35, 44, 66-67, 87 top, 88, 89, 92-93, 96-97 (Jeff Foott); 15 bottom, 57 (Charles & Sandra Hood); 88-89, 138 top left (Johnny Johnson); 76-77 (Luiz Claudio Marigo); 42-43 (Hans Reinhard); 114 (Christian Zuber)

The Environmental Picture Library Ltd: 145 (Roger Grace)

Stephen Gooder: 37, 39, 40, 50

Mary Evans Picture Library: 12, 13, 14, 68 top left

Ffotograff: 107 top right (Charles Aithie)

Jack Jackson: 21, 47

Ned Middleton: 27

NHPA: 87 bottom left, 143 (A.N.T./Kelvin Aitken); 87 bottom right (A.N.T.); 152-153 (Henry Ausloos); 19 (Patrick Fagot); 135 (John Hayward); 78 (Rich Kirshner); 2, 94 (Gerard Lacz); 33 (Jany Sauvanet); 75 (Kevin Schafer),

Oxford Scientific Films: 90-91 (Tony Bomford); 80-81 (David B. Fleetham); 112, 138-139 (Howard Hall); 127 (Mike Hill); 34 (Gregory Ochocki); 134 (James D. Watt); 128 (Norbet Wu)

Planet Earth Pictures: 121 (Ken Lucas); 99 (Doug Perrine); 110 (Peter Scoones); 31 (James D. Watt)

Still Pictures: 25; 119 (H. Ausloss); 30, 33 top left, 144 (Mark Carawardine); 37 top right (Christophe Guinet); 130 (Michel Gunter); 131 (Bruno Mazodier); 15 top right, 20 (J.P. Sylvestre)

Survival Anglia Ltd: 48-49, 146-147 (Jeff Foott)

Tigress Productions Limited: 124 (Doug Allan); 126

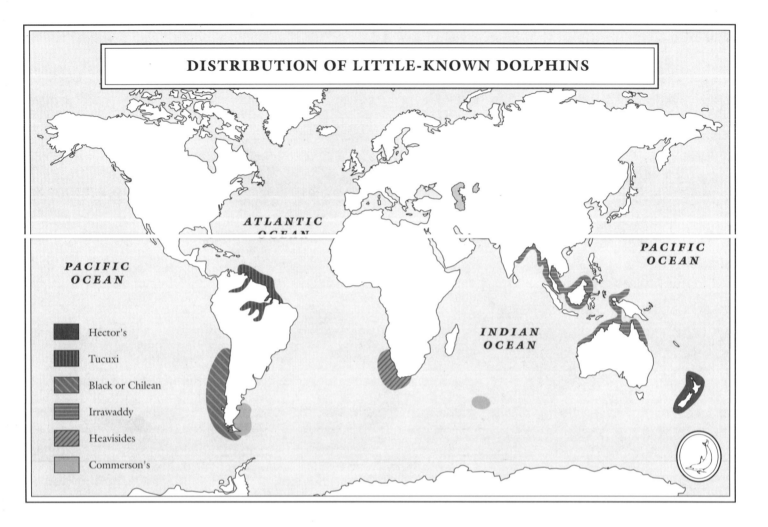

DISTRIBUTION OF LITTLE-KNOWN DOLPHINS

ATLANTIC OCEAN

PACIFIC OCEAN

PACIFIC OCEAN

INDIAN OCEAN

- Hector's
- Tucuxi
- Black or Chilean
- Irrawaddy
- Heavisides
- Commerson's

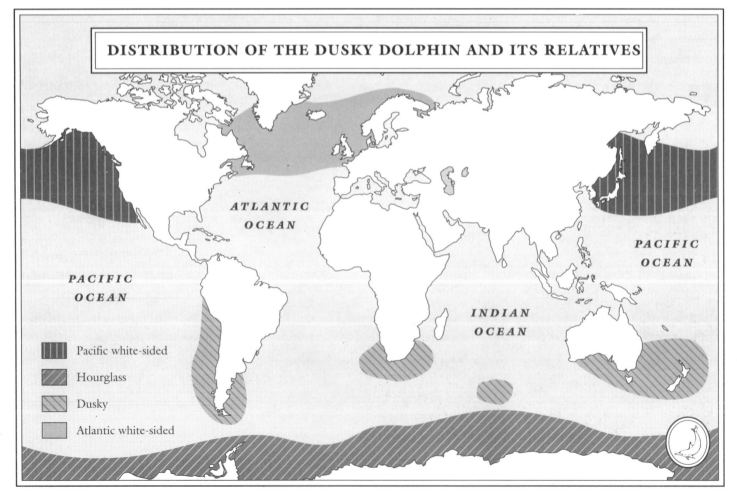

DISTRIBUTION OF THE DUSKY DOLPHIN AND ITS RELATIVES

ATLANTIC OCEAN

PACIFIC OCEAN

PACIFIC OCEAN

INDIAN OCEAN

- Pacific white-sided
- Hourglass
- Dusky
- Atlantic white-sided